The Beauty of Aging

A Woman's Guide to Joyful Living

ANGELA PAUL

iUniverse, Inc.
New York   Bloomington

The Beauty of Aging
A Woman's Guide to Joyful Living

Copyright © 2009 Angela M. Paul

iUniverse books may be ordered through booksellers or by contacting:

iUniverse
1663 Liberty Drive
Bloomington, IN 47403
www.iuniverse.com
1-800-Authors (1-800-288-4677)

ISBN: 978-0-595-44683-4 (pbk)
ISBN: 978-0-595-89006-4 (ebk)

Printed in the United States of America

iUniverse rev. date: 4/30/2009

For my mum Kathleen who taught me that a little vanity goes a long way,
and for my daughter Arielle who fills me with joy.

Acknowledgements

Special thanks to Arielle for the many long hours, editorial advice and youthful insights that helped shape this book. I will never forget the laughter and tears we shared along the way. My deep gratitude to my husband Alan for his unceasing love, encouragement and patient technical support. Much love and many thanks to my dad Tom, my brother Martin, my sister Sharon and my step-mum Jean for always being there for me. Thanks to Debbie and Pam for their friendship and support and to all the amazing women in my life who inspire me every day. Thanks to Joan Allen for her fabulous photography and Lina Barr for the beautiful cover design. As always I am grateful to Divine Mother for everything.

CONTENTS

Introduction

Last week I watched two pop icons, Cher and Tina Turner, being interviewed together by Oprah. Oprah asked them both this big question: "how do you feel about getting older?" Cher, now sixty-one, quickly and candidly replied, "I think it sucks." Then, the sixty-eight-year old Tina responded quite differently, "I welcome it with open arms, because my senior life is so much better than when I was young … you don't mind being sixty-eight, number doesn't mean a thing—it just doesn't." My guess is that when it comes to *getting older*, most midlife American women probably fall somewhere between Cher and Tina Turner's take on aging.

Personally, I think it's a great time to be a woman in her fifties. I would never trade the poise and confidence I have gained over the years for the looks and insecurities of my youth. Would you? It took every one of those fifty-three years to feel the way I do now. I value every year I have lived, and I love the woman I am becoming. I am no longer a girl, nor do I desire to be one.

I also do not *feel bad about my neck* or any other body part for that matter. It's not that my body is free from saggy flesh or parts that need some serious lifting; it's just that age has brought with it the unexpected gift of self-love and self-acceptance. This is priceless to me. I am more at ease in my own skin than I was at twenty-five or even forty. I have grown to be a woman with more depth than I ever dreamed I was capable of, and let me tell you—that is such a wonderful, long-awaited surprise. Sure, it has also brought with it wrinkles, creaky joints, and hair that grows in some unwanted places.

But at the end of the day, however, our aging experiences, like anything else in life, will be determined by our perceptions of it. It's pointless to keep striving for outer beauty without addressing the deeper need to examine how we think. Despite our fervent attempts to deny our aging, every year we all get older. The issue is whether you are going to get *old*.

The problem for many women is that they get old in their heads first. Aging is a natural part of life, so the sooner you can relax and accept that fact, the more pleasurable your experience of aging will be. Yes, at times it may also be fraught with some of the hard stuff in life, but that's just part and parcel of the human experience.

This is what I know—life is short and over far too soon. I do not have time to worry and obsess about something I ultimately have no control over. I prefer to use that energy instead to enjoy the life I am still fortunate to have. By the time we reach fifty, most of us have been through our share of challenges and losses, but in the big scheme of things, I don't count the loss of my youth as one of them. In fact, I'm grateful to be here at all. My health is pretty much intact, and my body continues to serve me well. And as for my less-than-perky boobs, I'm just glad I still have them. I have friends and family who haven't been so fortunate.

I have not let go of my vanities, however, nor do I intend to. I'll probably still be shaving my legs at eighty and searching for the best push-up brassiere to lift my girls. I enjoy the outer frivolities and indulgencies that make me feel good and help to deflect time a bit. But the beauty secret that serves me the most is the knowledge that while superficial beauty fades over time, beauty derived from wisdom, joy, experience, and humor does not. This is what sets us apart from the generations behind us who have not yet figured it out.

It's not about whether you can compete in the looks department with a woman a decade younger than you—that's easy these days with Botox, fillers, and all sorts of cosmetic surgical procedures. I'm talking about the light and glow in your smile and the intelligence and laughter in your eyes. It's about the confidence that comes from knowing who you are in the deepest sense. That's what sets us apart.

We can live brainwashed by our youth-obsessed society into believing that beauty is reserved only for the young. I beg to differ. There is beauty in our aging. I staunchly believe that beauty has no age limit. I see it in the amazing women I observe everyday. I see it in you and I see it in me. We may live in bodies that age, but our souls are ageless. And if you take care of yourself from the inside out, your mind can be as young as you want it to be.

So what does it take to live joyfully as we age? We need to free our minds, love our bodies, and nourish our spirits. With those principles in mind, *The Beauty of Aging* is divided into three sections. I start with "A Makeover for Your Mind" because without the inner work of changing our outdated perceptions of aging, then no amount of primping the outer self is going to bring lasting joy and self-esteem. We'll also look at how the sensual delights of pleasure and great sex start in the mind and go a long way in keeping us vibrant and young. Once you free your mind, then it's onto "Love Your Body," where we look at body image, self-care, and tips on healthy eating, exercise, sleep, and of course, all those fun beauty "secrets" I've stored up over the years.

In the last section "Nourish Your Spirit," we get to explore the healing benefits of meditation, faith, service, and the transformative power of silence and solitude. We will also look at the many aspects of love, including one of my favorite topics, marriage. Believe me, I have a lot to say on that! I conclude with "Death and Immortality" because I am a firm believer that in order to live well and fully, we have to come to terms with that white elephant in the room, formally known as death.

The possibility to be healthy, happy, and beautiful at midlife and beyond is available to each of us now more than ever before. All you have to do to start is to know it, believe it, and live it. *The Beauty of Aging* will show you how. My wish is that my book will help you feel your most beautiful ever and inspire you each day to fall in love with the radiant woman you have become.

> *One is not born a woman, one becomes one.*

—Simone De Beauvoir

A Makeover for Your Mind

Accept and Embrace Your Aging

Let the world know you as you are, because sooner or later, if you are posing,
you will forget the pose, and then where will you be?

—Fanny Brice

There is a time for the loveliness of youth and a time for the beauty of aging. Beauty does not belong only to the young. If you can learn to relax with where you are right now, instead of being futilely attached to your youth, a softening will occur that will not only melt away your anxiety and fear of aging, but will actually make you appear younger and more radiant.

Paying careful attention to what is going on in my mind seems to do more for my complexion than any face cream. Would it be lovely if I could have the looks of, say, my late twenties, as well as the wisdom and confidence I have today? Since that will never happen, not in this lifetime anyway, it seems like a silly waste of time to even go there. I prefer to focus on the time that I am fortunate to have right now. Age may bring some undesirable physical changes, but it also brings the bonus of increased emotional and psychological wellness.

The more we resist aging, we actually age more.

As with most experiences in life, the more we resist change, the more painful and challenging the experience of change becomes. Worrying about something we ultimately have little control over only adds more wrinkles and stress, which then makes us look older—the very thing we are trying to avoid. The more we resist our natural aging process—instead of embracing the inevitable changes that come with the passing years—the more desperate and fearful we become.

I regard aging as a Triumph, a result of strength and survivorship.

—Margaret Kuhn

Even with this new understanding, aging can still at times be anxiety provoking and overwhelming. We plod along making the best of it with as much dignity and grace as we can muster. I don't know any woman who wakes up one morning and sees her wrinkles and loose flesh in the mirror and exclaims, "Wow, I just love that I look older, and I can't wait to have even more wrinkles and sagging flesh." No, it's not quite like that for most women, myself included.

I see my aging and thank God it has happened gradually, but there is no denying it. Nor do I want to most of the time. At a certain point, we have to acknowledge that our youth is gone and no matter how much external work we do on ourselves, it will not come back. There is a sense of loss as our forties roll into our fifties and on into our sixties. For me, my fifties still feel young, but how will I feel when sixty lurks around the corner? I can live in a state of dread or welcome the birth of a new chapter in my life. I can cling to the youth of my past or get on with making the most of the gift of life I have left.

Most men will tell you that confidence in a woman is very appealing, whereas obsessive fear over one's aging is a definite turn-off. Embracing and accepting your age does not mean that you allow yourself to be defined by a calendar number or the opinions and judgments thrust *Beauty does not belong solely to the young.* upon you by a society that worships youth. It does mean that when you stand strong in who you are, and what you have learned as a woman at the height of your power, then midlife, with all it's scary and unknown terrain, has the promise and potential to be the best time in your life.

> *Aging ain't for sissies.*
> —Bette Davis

Still, American women fear aging for good reason. In our society, we do not value the beauty of a woman growing into her own skin. Society and the media tell us that wrinkles and a less-than-svelte body are not beautiful or desirable, so it is no wonder that many women feel almost invisible once they reach midlife. It takes a strong mind, courage, and fierce determination to resist the continuous onslaught of negative messages thrown at us by a youth-biased media and culture.

Fortunately for today's midlife woman, we are moving into an era where old stereotypes no longer apply nor are tolerated. According to a 2006 Dove Global Study, "Beauty Comes of Age," 97 percent of American women believe it is time for America to change its views about women and aging, and 93 percent of women globally believe misconceptions exist about women over fifty in society.

Be honest about your age

The first step to personal freedom is to be honest about your biological age. When I was chosen to be on the cover of *More* magazine, it was very liberating to have my age printed in black and white for all to see. But the truth is it was also startling. I looked at the number and

I just couldn't believe that it was really my age. Fifty. Not that I was worried or self-conscious about revealing the truth of my age, I just couldn't equate how I feel inside with the number fifty.

Confidence is sexy and alluring, desperate clinging to one's youth is not.

Where, we ask ourselves as we reach midlife, did all that time go? How can I possibly be fifty? As a child the age fifty sounded positively geriatric. I decided it was just a number and nothing more. It's a waste of time to fixate on numbers that only serve to make us feel bad. I actually enjoy seeing the surprise on people's faces when I am asked my age and give them the true answer. Will I feel the same way when I turn sixty? I'll let you know when I get there.

I have a girlfriend who says she stopped counting once she hit fifty-five. She still celebrates her birthday, but when asked how old she is, she simply says she's a year older than she was last year and leaves it at that. I must say part of me sees the appeal and temptation in this kind of approach. It's not quite denial, but it veers very close. I hope that at sixty I will still be staunchly honest about my age, but I reserve the right to change my mind on this if I so choose.

To me, old age is always 15 years older than I am.

—Bernard Baruch

I feel young, but I have the confidence that only comes from age and experience. My idea of fifty and that of many of my friends is extremely different from our mothers' midlife experiences. I never expected to feel as vibrant and sensual at fifty as I do now, and I hope that will continue well into my sixties and beyond.

The more we mid-age women are able to step forward and own our true age, the further we advance in freeing ourselves and each other from the social stereotypes of how midlife should look. We are living at a time when we have infinite resources and information to enhance the quality of our lives if we so choose. But it's hard to move forward if you succumb to the pressure to

If a guy has an issue with your age, then he simply isn't worth a minute of your valuable time.

lie about your age. If you hope to triumph over the repressive myth of aging, you need to start by being honest about your age. Only then can you stand with your feminine queenly power and wisdom and reflect to the world that there most definitely is beauty in aging.

If I am fortunate, one day I will be an elder, and I hope to embrace that stage of life with serenity, grace, and the same passion and enthusiasm as I embrace my midlife with. I may still be lifting weights at eighty, but I don't think I'll be interested in practicing the hundred positions of Tantric sex (then again, who knows?) or waste the time I have left fussing over my looks. I hope to always feel young and healthy, but will no longer be interested in looking young and sexy. Instead, I look forward to the unique treasures, grace, and growth that every passage of life affords.

I was grown up at ten, and first began to grow young at forty.

—Madge Kendal

The next step is to rejoice at reaching midlife and celebrate it with friends who honor aging instead of fearing it. When I celebrate birthdays with my girlfriends, we constantly reinforce each other with positive messages like *another year older and better* or *the best is yet to come,* instead of dragging out so-called humorous outdated slogans like *fifty and over the hill.* Some women say they stop celebrating their birthday once they reach forty. What a pity. I love birthdays and see them as a blessed opportunity to celebrate my life, my loved ones, and myself. My women friends who have triumphed over serious illness celebrate their birthdays with an extra wattage of joy and gratitude. They are grateful to be still alive and know they can never take a day for granted.

Denial of your age can only go so far and buys into the notion that aging is bad.

With each new year you can choose to age with dignity and grace. You may not be particularly fond of the age spots and wrinkles you have earned on your short journey through life, but they are part of you. If you can't love them, at least learn to accept them.

Who are some of the women you admire?

Bold, confident women across the country and around the globe are breaking out of the old mold and blazing the way for younger women to follow. To help to make this journey the best you can, look for and cultivate positive role models. Try to find role models who reflect your values. You could make a list of women your age or older whom you admire. Include family, friends, celebrities, politicians, community, or world leaders.

It's also good to read books or articles about older women you respect or find inspiring. And you might want to cut out magazine pictures of midlife and older women whom you find beautiful, sexy, or attractive. Make a collage of them on poster board or in your journal.

Women may be the one group that grows more radical with age.

—Gloria Steinem

A good way to integrate role models into your life is to schedule a weekly date or long phone conversation with a friend who is your age or older. Two of my many older friends I love talking to are Joan Tinei and Deborah Rogosin. Joan is in her eighties, and Deborah will turn seventy-five years young next year. Both are amazing women who celebrate each day with curiosity and enthusiasm. Among other things, Joan was married to a Samoan chief, sang the role of the cook in *Alice in Wonderland* for an opera company, and delivered babies.

These days she also works as an actress, landlady, and Sunday school teacher for teens. My fellow Aquarian Deborah is a licensed marriage and family therapist who has a huge heart and a sharp mind. Although she is now legally blind, Deborah is constantly up to something new, like teaching Braille to kids.

At the 2007 Oscars, we saw not one but three midlife actresses nominated in the best actress category including the winner, the ravishing Helen Mirren, sexy as ever at sixty-one.

Age is about attitude, not a number.

Last year, the radiant Julie Christie was a stand out in the movie *Away From Her*. I also look to Isabella Rossellini with her European sensibility and intelligence as my model and inspiration for aging well. I think that the lines on their faces add to their refined beauty and make them stand out in a business where most celebrities over thirty-five never seem to age at all.

I also love Mary Gordon, Jhumpa Lahiri, Toni Morrison, Mary Oliver, Pema Chodron, and Joyce Carol Oates for uplifting my spirit with their rapturous words. And Oprah for, well, just being Oprah and inspiring women all over the world to be the best they can be. Like many women, I am grateful to Dr. Christianne Northrup, Dr. Susan Love, and Suzanne Sommers for providing much-needed information and encouragement on menopause. Joni Mitchell, for the guts and courage to keep on making beautiful and meaningful music in an industry that cares more about image than talent.

Joni Mitchell's "Both Sides Now" was my favorite song as a teen. I don't know why, but even then it moved me to tears. Now that I've reached my fifties, her more recent sultry version of the song moves me even deeper.

I've looked at life from both sides now, from win and lose, and still somehow, it's life's illusions I recall, I really don't know life at all.

—Joni Mitchell

And regardless of what your political leaning may be, 2008 was the year that Hillary Clinton had a real shot at becoming America's first female president. America is still behind in this area. For example, in the 1990s, Margaret Thatcher was Britain's prime minister for two terms. In Israel, Golda Meir was the first woman to be elected prime minister and the third woman in the world to hold this office. Obviously, we still have some catching up to do; however we are making strides.

For me, another recent highlight was the historic sight of Nancy Pelosi raising the gravel as America's first female Speaker of the House. There she was with all her grandchildren joining her on the podium for that celebratory moment in *her*-story. We also had Condoleeza Rice as the United States' first African American woman to serve as secretary of state. Imagine in the future how many more women in top political positions we may have leading this country.

Beauty as a commodity

Beauty as a commodity is bound to disappear. If a woman's self-worth is determined by how she looks, then she will have a very difficult time when those looks inevitably fade. There are many physically beautiful women who are deeply insecure and become more so as they age. I know this from my own experience as a young model many years ago. The modeling business isn't exactly the best business for fostering real self-esteem. It's a world in which rejection and competition go hand in hand.

I learned, as most models do, not to take rejection personally. It still hurt. I also witnessed the anxiety and panic of older models who knew that their careers were on a downward slope once they hit twenty-five or so, as they were soon to be replaced by fresh new faces.

In the pre-Botox days, I remember one "older model" of twenty-four who would show up for work with her forehead covered in white tape so she wouldn't be able to frown. As soon as the job was done, she would stick the tapes back on her forehead. Other models lived on a diet of caffeine and cigarettes as well as more serious drugs to stay thin and trim.

Healthy self-esteem is a direct result of self-love and self-respect. Self-love is unconditional acceptance of oneself—flaws and defects included. Self-respect is about the choices we make, and self-esteem is the outcome. Each time we make a loving healthy choice for ourselves, we develop confidence and self-esteem.

The kind of confidence I am talking about comes from age, clarity, and experience. Looking good is a by-product of self-esteem and not, in my experience, the cause. I take pride in my appearance, but I am not interested in the false confidence that is dependent on the fickle opinion and approval of others. Great looks fade over time, but confidence and beauty that comes from the inside does not.

> *Youth and beauty do not promise confidence and self-esteem.*

> *Only simplicity and the truth count.*
> *It has to come from the inside. You can't fake it.*
>
> —Audrey Hepburn

As for my early modeling career, I quit at the ripe old age of twenty-six with more good memories than not. And who would have thought that I would actually be getting back into modeling at fifty, thanks to the More/Wilhelmina 40+ Model Search Contest. But it's a whole different experience this time around, with a new market geared to women my age. It's more about being healthy instead of being thin and young. I get to be myself, so there isn't the same kind of pressure.

This is what I have learned: how I feel on the inside means more to me than wrinkle-free skin. I take good care of myself, but I don't obsess. That's the key. I find that by focusing on things in my life that enrich me from the inside out, I have less time to obsess about the outside. I enjoy life and all it brings, and I believe that shows up on my face.

Your best life is now

Your midlife is a golden opportunity to begin this next stage of life with excitement and a sense of adventure, opening up to all the possibilities and joy that aging can bring. The wisdom of life experience and the clarity and perspective it offers is just one of the many assets of aging. But to age gracefully, we need good health and a positive attitude—not so easy to come by when we live in a culture that rewards the fruits of youthful beauty and lives in fear of aging. Here's a perfect example. In a 2006 edition of *More* magazine, editor in chief Peggy Northrup recalled the story of a gorgeous over forty blonde actress who was dropped by her agent because her age was printed along with her picture as is customary in *More*.

It's up to each one of us to do our part to move beyond this old and limiting mode of thinking, and create a life free from the confines and restrictions that may have held women back in the past. Isn't it time to stop letting others dictate how we should live our lives? Rules are meant to be broken, especially when they do nothing but limit us from being more of who we can be.

My eighty-two-year-old friend Joan recently finished her first book and is currently performing in a dance troupe on a major cruise line. She lives life by *her* rules and nobody else's. That's another plus to aging: you begin to experience the freedom that comes when you care less about what people think of you.

During much of my life, I was anxious to be what someone else wanted me to be.
Now I have given up the struggle. I am what I am.

—Elizabeth Coatsworth

Dignity or Donald Duck lips?

Clinging to false youth at any cost takes away the dignity of the natural passages and cycles of life. Experience, confidence, wisdom, insight, and appreciation of life cannot be bought in a jar of the latest anti-wrinkle cream or cosmetic surgery. They are free, however, for any woman who is ready to make some positive choices and create a better life for herself from the inside out. This means we have to take responsibility and change what's in our power to enhance the quality of our own aging experience.

As for the issue of cosmetic surgery, it definitely stirs up mixed feelings of judgment and fascination. We simultaneously judge others while fantasizing about our own imagined makeover. A little discreet nip and tuck may well boost a woman's confidence temporarily, if she is doing it for the right reasons, can find a great surgeon, and then knows when to stop.

I avoid any kind of surgery as much as possible, so I'm not about to let anyone put a knife to my face even if I am knocked out. Besides that, surgery scares me because it is so final. What if I hate it and it's too late, and I end up looking like an alien with a face and eyes that don't move and lips like Donald Duck. That is just not beautiful to me, and I don't think it is to men either. Why do so many women buy into the illusion that a taut, expressionless face is beautiful? Could it be that one day we will get to the point where a surgically untouched face will become the exception and therefore seen as beautiful once again? Wouldn't that be refreshing!

Everything will change. The only question is growing up or decaying.

—Nikki Giovanni

The risk with cosmetic surgery is that when the initial flush has faded, some women feel the need to get more and more work done and end up addicted to the scalpel of the Michael Jackson–Joan Rivers School of cosmetic surgery. I know that the business of Hollywood can be harsher on aging actresses than men, but honestly some actresses look so bizarre that you have to wonder, what were they thinking? And besides aren't actresses suppose to show expression when they act?

When you are joyful and excited by life, your face magically appears more youthful and refreshed.

It's the same problem with the liberal overuse of Botox. Small amounts of Botox applied by a reputable skillful doctor can make a huge difference, especially in the frown line between the brow. Too much, however, may result in an unnatural surprised look. Even worse, when administered incorrectly, Botox can result in a frozen brow or droopy eyelid. If you opt for Botox, be sure to use a qualified doctor, and for quality control stay away from spas or Botox parties. And remember, less is definitely more. The goal is to help soften expression lines while still retaining movement in your face.

With the rare exception, many celebrities would have us believe that their unlined faces are the result of excellent genes, not Botox or the work of a skilled surgeon. That said, in 2007, over 4.3 million women got Botox, and I'm sure they're not all celebrities or fashion insiders living in Los Angeles or New York. For the record, I have used Botox and been pleased with the results. Getting a little Botox a couple of times a year is a frivolity I allow myself, and not a big deal to me.

On days when my reflection in the mirror looks old and tired, I, like many women, have the fleeting fantasy of imagining how much younger I could look if the breasts and the eyelids were lifted upward, instead of their downward descent. Alas, Botox does not remedy these particular concerns. At the same time, I am grateful that I am blessed with the genes of good skin and high cheekbones. But as for as the droopy breasts, well, one can do miracles with a push up brassiere. Don't you just love that word? Brassiere!

Most of us want to look natural, whatever that means these days. Oh, but what time and effort goes into looking natural! Many celebrities would like you to believe that they wake up in the morning looking naturally gorgeous. That might be the case if you are under twenty-five, but the rest of us have to put some effort into looking good. How much time and effort is delegated is up to the individual. I for one don't want to look like I tried too hard.

I have everything now that I had twenty years ago,
except now it's all lower.

—Gypsy Rose Lee

Trying too hard is a turn-off, not a turn-on

It's sad to witness so many women living in despair over their aging. What is all the panic about? My friend Amy is an attractive, intelligent woman who is not in despair about her aging, and still she says that turning sixty next year is daunting and terrifying for her. She says that though she doesn't feel old herself, it is others' response to her age that disturbs her.

Are we so afraid that we will no longer be able to ignite the fire of lust and desire in the opposite sex that we will go to any extreme to look young and sexy?

Unfortunately, there are still too many people in the world, especially men, who are stuck on numbers. For Amy, withholding her age is not an option, so it is interesting to see how she navigates her way through this transition. I may be a decade behind her, but I know how fast time passes. Our life circumstances may be different, but we learn from those who go before us. I know that if any one can triumph over social labeling and come out shining, she can.

But what is it that makes some otherwise smart and self-assured women strut around attempting to mimic a twenty-year-old in the latest fashion fads? Ugg boots and miniskirts should only be worn by a sixteen-year-old. Great style is ageless, but going out looking like mutton dressed as lamb (one of my mum's favorite sayings) with super low-cut jeans, bare midriff, and bright-colored thongs should be banned.

Hopefully there comes a point in a woman's maturing where being considered sexy is not a major priority and she has the insight to realize that trying a little too hard becomes a turn-off rather than a turn-on. Sexy is about attitude and confidence, not how short your skirt is or how low your neckline. I don't go out looking for male attention, but I would be lying if I said it didn't feel good to still turn a few male heads when I pass by—especially if the men are a lot younger than me. Will I feel sad when it gradually happens less and less? Probably. But I also hope to have a wistful mature acceptance of the positive attributes of my aging: fond memories, healthy loving relationships, and a rich and fulfilling life that affords me the clarity to appreciate what is truly meaningful and important.

Who says that a woman can't be sexy at fifty and beyond?

In American society, we have been programmed into accepting a narrow view of what and who is sexy and beautiful. In Europe, Charlotte Rampling with her heavy hooded eyes is still considered seductive at sixty, and Sophia Loren at seventy recently posed in lingerie for a well-known European pin up calendar. One attractive friend of mine who is fifty-five is reluctant to tell midlife men her real age, for fear of immediate rejection. Another radiant friend at fifty-nine tells me that, ironically, sex with a young lover is more easygoing and free than with a man her own age. It's not about sexual stamina and performance; it's the ability of the young lover to appreciate her ripe sensuality and beauty without going through a mind trip about her age.

There's a fabulous scene in the movie *Something's Gotta Give* (2004) where Frances McDormant goes off into a great rant addressing the fact that some older men seem to be only interested in dating younger women. It's a brilliantly witty scene, sharp and to the point. When Jack Nicholson falls in love with Diane Keaton, the mother of the young woman he's been dating, he finally wakes up to what he's been missing all the years courting women decades younger than he.

Age doesn't matter unless you're a cheese.

—Billy Burke

Why do some older men reject strong, accomplished midlife women? Perhaps these men feel challenged and inferior to them. That would explain why they date or marry younger trophy wives, who are less intimidating and challenging. On the other hand, European men, such as the French or Italians, are often more refined in their taste. Age isn't usually an issue to them. They know and appreciate the finer things in life: food, wine, and the pleasures of a luscious, confident woman.

Remember, we teach others, especially men, how to treat us.

If you happen to be in the singles market, I hope that the men you are dating are treating you like the goddesses you are. If not, you are selling yourself short. Fortunately, there is also a contingent of hip young men who prefer to date older women. One young man I know who loves to date older women said there is something deeper behind the eyes, a knowing and intelligence, a sense of intrigue and poise that is lacking in younger women.

I'm not suggesting that you take a young lover—though that might be a fun and interesting thing to do if you are so inclined. The important thing is to choose men who are worthy of being with an amazing, remarkable woman like you whatever their age.

Dealing with the hard stuff

Come celebrate with me that every day something has tried to kill me and has failed.

—Lucille Clifton

As we reach midlife we will also have to deal with some of the most difficult challenges of aging. We need to accept and embrace them too. You may begin to notice that death, illness, and transitions are all around you. Many of us are dealing with sick aged parents, and at the same time are trying to get our kids into the best college, or at least make it through high school. Some things in life we simply must go through.

I went through my own experience with this about three years ago. It was an intense time of many losses, the most painful being the death of my beloved mum, Kathleen. In the short space of about six months, my sister-in-law and mother-in-law died, my father had to undergo major heart surgery, my only child left for college, and shortly after that my mum died.

Nothing in my life had prepared me for the pain of watching my mum slowly loose her mind to dementia. It was gut wrenching not to be able to help her when she did not know who she was, never mind who my dad and I were. In the early stages of the disease, she was terrified of the strange unfamiliar voices in her head and the images of deceased loved ones who kept showing up to talk to her. She became increasingly hostile to my dad and fretted that gangs of bad people were trying to break into the house. Some nights after dinner she would put her hat and coat on and say that she had to leave and catch the bus to go home to her husband.

Losing your mum is especially hard for a woman, no matter what age you're at, or what quality of relationship you may have had.

Once when I was visiting, she grabbed my hand really tightly and cried out "Angela, I'm so scared. I just want to feel like myself again." I held her securely in my arms as she once held me when I was a child and told her she was going to be okay. I was not okay and did not believe she would be either.

Over time, as the disease progressed, she began to spend more time in this *alternate* reality and less time in the *real* world. She became more at ease and less afraid. She spoke little, and when she did it was, more often than not, nonsensical. At least to her caregivers it was. I felt her peace and knew she was okay, and no longer enduring the cruel mental suffering that had earlier on terrorized her mind. I was glad about that. Sometimes, though, I really wanted her to know and see me instead of looking through me. Even harder were the days when she would not open her eyes at all.

I remember one particular morning when I was preparing to leave for the airport after an extended stay to help my dad take care of her. I knelt on the bed crying and told her I loved her so much, but had to leave now. I wanted her to look me in the eye and tell me she loved me too. I kept on trying to rouse her attention, but she would not open her eyes and look at me. I was leaving, but she had already left.

A woman is like a tea bag—you never know how strong she is until she gets in hot water.

—Eleanor Roosevelt

When I look back on it now, I wonder how I found the strength and courage to get through it all. We do when we have no other choice. It doesn't require much courage or substance on our part when things are going well in life; it's when we are faced with serious problems and numbing loss that we begin to experience bravery and courage in a whole new life-sustaining way.

How could this be? It's hard to explain. But even with all the sorrow and sadness, a part of me was able to accept and see that it was an inevitable part of life. It was the most achingly painful time in my life, but it was also the most rich and beautiful. The support of my loving family and my deep connection to Spirit helped me through. It is during times of intense emotional challenges like this that we rely on grace—grace that heals our hearts and helps to soften the blows.

I allowed myself the space and time to grieve like I had never experienced before in my life. I cried on and off for a good year. Even now, when I see an elderly woman at the market who reminds me of my mum, I am taken aback by the sadness I still feel and the tears I still shed. Every time I think of her, I feel her presence. I do not want that to ever end.

There is no way to avoid these changes and losses. The best we can do is be gentle, loving, and kind to ourselves at these most difficult times. We need to reach out to family, friends, and our spiritual community if we have one. For me, it was the perfect opportunity to allow myself to be vulnerable, when in the past I took pride in being the one people came to for encouragement or support. I learned that it takes strength to let go and ask for help. I also learned that most people are delighted at the opportunity to comfort and give, if we just ask.

In youth we learn, in age we understand.

—Marie Ebner Eshenbach

While loss of any kind is difficult, don't let life slip away by living in the past. Why miss out on all the treasures to be found right here and now in the midlife you are fortunate to have. Everyone has to go through times of pain and challenge; they're part of the amazing and sometimes mysterious journey of life. If something is not working in your life and you have the power to change it, do so. You can begin by celebrating midlife and by being grateful for what you have and what you know.

A face and eyes that glow with intelligence, kindness, and the serenity derived from a life well lived is a gift of beauty to be beheld. When you are at ease in your skin and you allow the radiance of your inner light to shine forth, you are beautiful. You have so much to bring to the world—don't limit yourself by living in fear and panic.

Learn to relax, let go, and smile. It will do more for you than a face-lift. And remember: even a sixteen-year-old will be sixty one day—if she's lucky.

What a wonderful life I've had!
I only wish I'd realized it sooner.

—Colette

YOU ARE AS YOUNG AS YOU THINK

Aging is mind over matter. If you don't mind, then it don't matter.

—Dolly Parton

All change begins with a single thought. To change your reality of aging, you must start with changing your perceptions. The adage *you are as young as you feel* might best be changed to *you are as young as you think.* When it comes to your health and aging, the body and mind are so profoundly connected that what you think eventually reflects back in your body. The power to affect your health and happiness is in your hands, or to be more precise, in your mind.

According to Deepak Chopra's philosophy on aging as explained in his best-seller, *Grow Younger, Live Longer*, you cannot change your chronological age—how old you are by the calendar—but you can change how old you feel—by changing your thinking. In turn, how well you take care of yourself will affect your biological age—how time and life has affected your organs making you susceptible to illness and decay. A fifty-five-year-old woman who has taken exceptional care of herself in the past may well have the biological age of a forty-year-old. The reverse also holds true—a woman who has neglected her health may have the biological age of a woman much older.

Emotions are our bodies' reactions to our minds

We begin to age the moment we are born, but how well you age depends on how well you take care of yourself. The truth is that lifestyle has more to do with how we age than genetics. Everyday we have the capacity to affect our physical, emotional, and mental health by how we think. If each day you tell yourself that you are old and unhealthy, how can you possibly feel young and fit? Growing old does not mean a progressive decline in mental and physical capabilities—unless you believe it to be so.

My gym is filled with women decades older than me who are still lifting weights and put me to shame with their sun salutations in my yoga class. I also know women much younger than me who constantly complain about how old they are getting, without doing a thing to change their self-sabotaging habits and negative thinking. We all get stuck in negative thought patterns at times, but we have the choice to decide which thoughts we are going to feed.

You can read books like this one, listen to tapes and attend seminars, and hear inspirational speakers tell you how to shift your life around. You can learn about the seven and ten steps to every kind of success you can imagine. You can find teachers, life coaches, and gurus, and it may all help. At the end of the day, however, you and you alone have to do the tough, yet ultimately liberating work to change your thinking so you can change your life for the good.

Health and wellness start within by the thoughts we think most of the time.

What thought has done, thought can undo.

—Ernest Holmes

It is not easy to clip the wires of past negative thought patterns. Habitual negative self-talk can get really comfortable. Change means risk, which can seem terrifying even when we know it's what we really need. Before you can do anything with your thoughts, you have to be aware of what you're thinking in the first place, instead of drifting through life on automatic pilot. When a problem seems impenetrable, let it go for a while. Come back to it later when your thoughts are clearer. From this place of calm, you will be able to arrive at a solution.

My meditation practice has helped me to become more aware of my thoughts, whether I am sitting in formal mediation or busy in my daily activities. During the course of the day, I like to stop what I am doing and focus on where my thoughts are at any given time. When my emotions get stirred up, I ask myself what's going on inside me right now. I am usually attached to some thought that is giving me unrest. The other day I caught myself ruminating over the fact that the biggest part of my life is over. Even if I live till my eighties, I told myself, I have less time ahead of me than behind me. Just thinking such thoughts made me feel depressed and old. Once I became aware of the mind trip I was on, I was able to let the thought go and the uncomfortable emotion along with it.

Everyone has difficulties to face in life, some more than others. I've indulged in a pity party for one at times, but it gets pretty lonely after a while. Sometimes life doesn't turn out the way we hope, and we all feel sorry for ourselves on occasion. Lingering in victim consciousness, however, never helps. I soon get sick of my own company when I'm wallowing in my whining. I don't like being around me, so I can't imagine why anyone else would either.

No magic wand

There is no magic wand you can wave that can take you from unhealthy to healthy. You can go on a fad diet and loose ten pounds, but once you go back to your old eating patterns, you'll put it right back on. If you feel disgusted with yourself after you've eaten that sixth slice of pizza or tub of Cold Stone ice cream, then don't eat it. Sorry ladies but discipline and self-control is the only way. Only you can do that for yourself. It's simple but powerful,

It isn't what goes on in your life that causes suffering, it's what goes on in your mind.

though granted, not always easy. If you succumb to temptation like we all do from time to time, just patiently and lovingly start over again.

Besides meditation, the practice of positive affirmations and visualization has been enormously helpful in my life. In order to erase the deeply etched tapes of judgmental thoughts endlessly swirling around in our minds, we have to replace those thoughts with loving, positive thoughts instead. There are no exact formulas for doing this. Find what works for you and stick with it. The important thing to remember with affirmations is that definitive statements generally produce definitive results. Know what you want, and then use words that are meaningful and true for you.

Here are a few affirmations that work for me:

- I am in perfect health and balance, and everything in my life is working out for my highest good.
- I am ageless and timeless and free from pain and suffering.
- I am safe and at peace, and all is well in my world.

The trouble with most women is they get old in their head.
They think about it too much.

—Josephine Baker

I don't think of myself as any particular age, though when I am tired, I sometimes feel ancient! I also no longer weigh myself. I can tell more about my health by how I feel than by a number on a scale. I know I am becoming more of myself in the deepest sense, and numbers could never express the fullness of how that looks and feels to me. I love these words of wisdom from 106-year-old California resident Magdelena Skiff, who states that "*106 is just a number. You can't think of it as growing old. You have to think of it as staying young.*"

Women in general are taking better care of their health than ever before and enjoying life more because of it. Your body and mind are inseparable, so protect your health by guarding your thoughts. Don't get old in your head! You are as young as you determine yourself to be. Do the work and reap the rewards. Women are making big and small changes every day, and so can you. Know you are worth your very best efforts, and then make your moves.

Letting go of the past

All the art of living lies in a fine mingling of letting go and holding on.

—Havelock Ellis

With age finally comes the understanding that we get to choose what to let go of and what is worth holding on to. Ask yourself which beliefs and memories benefit your future and which are best left in the past where they belong? Or another way to view it, to paraphrase Einstein, goes like this: "Insanity is repeating the same thing over and over and expecting a different result." If you continue to skip exercise and eat unhealthy but expect to lose weight, it will not happen. You are wasting your time. If you blame others for your lot in life while continuing to make poor personal choices, you are deluding yourself.

On the other hand, if you did not take good care of yourself in the past, today you can start anew to create a healthier you and a brighter tomorrow. Let go of old, self-defeating perceptions of yourself, and make the conscious choice to begin again. This requires that we spend some time visiting the past in order to move beyond it. Until we do that, despite our best efforts and intentions, we will keep getting stuck in the same destructive thought patterns and habits that prevent us from moving forward.

For many years, an acquaintance of mine had the self-defeating habit of choosing romantic relationships with men who derived pleasure in demeaning her. It wasn't until she began to explore why she chose such men that she was able to then choose a healthy relationship. It didn't take much analysis to understand that having a father who abandoned her as a child could result in poor choices in men when she became an adult. Even with this understanding and a new sense of compassion for herself, it still came down to the fact that only she could change her thoughts, actions, and ultimately her life.

There are years that ask questions and years that answer.

—Zora Neale Hurston

I have seen women look literally decades younger when they shed a past that has held them back. For some women, it will take a lot of courage to break out of old patterns. Sometimes it may be a seemingly small step like committing to get to sleep earlier each night or not eating after 7:00 p.m. Or it could be the hugely significant step of ending a long but unhealthy marriage. Sometimes we are ready for a change but are unsure of what that change looks like. You can brainstorm with a friend to come up with ideas, write in your journal, or best of all, in my experience, get comfortable with not knowing for a while. Fall in love with uncertainty, and in time, from the place of stillness and wisdom inside you, the answers will emerge.

Ask yourself the question: What do I need to know and do to create the life I really want?

When you think about the future, be sure that it is your dream you are hoping to fulfill— not someone else's. Women have often been conditioned to think about what others want first before themselves. The first step is to learn to think for yourself. We always hope someone else has the answer, but you know who you are, and you know what you want. You just have to trust in your wisdom, power, and strength.

You can expect that when you start to think for yourself, you will begin to rattle the boat a bit, especially if those closest to you are not used to you verbalizing your needs. Don't worry. They'll get used to it and may even welcome it. Some will be happy for you while others won't. At this point, you may have to reassess where you are going and whom you are taking with you.

The events of childhood do not pass, but repeat themselves
like seasons of the year.

—Eleanor Farjeon

Letting go of the past may mean letting go of certain people who do not support your highest potential and best interests. Think of the people in your life who encourage and uplift you. These are generally well-adjusted, positive folks who feel good about their own lives and want the best for you too.

Now think of the people who seem intent on bringing you down and suck the very life out of you. These toxic vampires are miserable in their own lives and want to pull you into the muck and mire of their negativity along with them. It doesn't take rocket science to figure out who's worthy of your company and who is not. The more you want health and happiness for yourself, the more you will attract people into your life who are *for* you and not *against* you. Some will want to hold you back, and others will want to pull you down. Let them go. If you allow people to treat you badly, that's what they will continue to do.

There is no third party out to get you. We harm ourselves the most by clinging to this false belief and alienate ourselves from others in the process. The interesting thing about life is it often shows up the way we expect it to. The universe corresponds by agreeing with what you believe. Expect goodness and grace, and you will attract it into your experience. Expect others to treat you poorly, and guess what, they will.

You are not the same person you were yesterday; every moment you are growing and evolving into someone new. No matter how difficult your past may have been, each new day you can begin again. You may also need to reach out to others for guidance and support. Find a wise therapist, reach out to a trusted friend, or seek out a spiritual counselor—whatever it takes to free your heart and mind.

I am larger, better than I thought. I did not know I held so much goodness.

—Walt Whitman

Remembering our goodness

When I am feeling down on myself, I try and remember at least one good thing from my past that I am proud of. Not a personal accomplishment per se, but an act of service toward someone. Once, when my daughter Arielle and I were driving in Malibu, we saw an elderly man running for the bus. Despite our efforts to stall the bus, the driver pulled away just as the elderly man made it to the stop. We saw how disappointed and exhausted he seemed after all the energy he put out, and we also knew that he'd probably have to wait a very long time before the next bus came. Without hesitating, Arielle turned to me and said that we should give the man a lift in our car to catch up with the bus. And that's just what we did.

To his surprise, we pulled up next to him, opened the car door, and told him to get in the back seat. He didn't speak English and our Spanish was pathetic, but his big grateful smile said everything. We zoomed off after the bus until it stopped about a half mile down the coast. We pulled up in front of the bus; he boarded and waved us good-bye. I felt good that Arielle and I were able to help the old man out, and I felt good that I had helped raise a child who cares deeply about others the way she does.

We all have aspects of our past that we would rather forget. Although the disappointments and regrets of the past may not be huge, they sometimes cast a shadow over our present reality. That is why memories and moments like the story above reaffirm the goodness that I believe is at the core of each one of us.

Never regret. If it's good, it's wonderful. If it's bad, it's experience.

—Victoria Holt

Forgiveness

There is no greater freedom from the past than when we learn to forgive. The inability to forgive festers in our body and can create havoc with our mental, physical, and emotional health. On a very rare occasion, I am able to forgive from a wise and altruistic perspective. But more often than not, it comes from a purely selfish desire to be free from painful emotions that rob me of the peace of mind I work hard to protect.

When the mind is obsessed with hatred and revenge, we can never be free from attachment to the person we are obsessing about. We will carry that person with us always, which is why forgiveness is so necessary to improve our emotional and mental health. It's impossible to age well when we hang on to a long list of people we want to get even with. You may want to punish the other person but end up hurting yourself. We can rationalize all we want that such a person doesn't deserve to be forgiven, but there is nothing sweet about revenge. It poisons the mind and makes us feel ugly inside, which in turn affects how we appear on the outside.

The weak can never forgive. Forgiveness is the attribute of the strong.

—Mahatma Gandhi

Years ago, a friend sent me one of those nasty letters we write in the heat of the moment but usually tear up or burn instead of actually sending. As I read her long emotional rant about my perceived flaws, I was furious that she chose to send me a letter instead of talking to me directly. At that time, I did not have the wisdom or maturity to try and look at the situation from her perspective. Soon after she called me and tried to make it right, but I was already so stuck in my self-righteous anger that I shut her out of my life and heart. I now regret that.

Some people are so bitter and so eaten up with the inability to forgive that you can actually see it in their faces.

I carried the burden of that anger and my inability to forgive for a long time until a few years later when I ran into her by *accident* at a local store. We spoke briefly about nothing in particular, but when I said good-bye and wished her well, I meant it. I did not know how I would respond to such an unplanned encounter though I had imagined similar situations in my head many times. After we spoke, I felt my heart open, and the weight of my long stored up anger and resentment lifted from me. What a relief.

Since that time, there have still been occasions when I have felt the sting of betrayal and the frustration of disappointment in relationships. That's life. I get over it better and faster. I still feel anger, but I don't allow myself to get lost in hatred and bitterness. Forgiveness takes courage and strength, and it takes time—sometimes longer than we would like. But when the heart has been badly pummeled, forgiveness cannot be rushed. Be gentle with yourself and take all the time you need.

It helps to remember, though, that even when forgiveness seems impossible, and certainly some people and acts seem unforgivable, that we forgive as a supreme act of loving kindness for ourselves. No one can take that from you unless you give away the permission to do so.

As long as you don't forgive, who and whatever it is will occupy rent free space in your mind.

—Isabelle Holland

GIVE YOURSELF OVER TO PLEASURE

Suddenly I awake to stark amazement at everything ...
To be alive is so incredible that all I can do is lie still and breathe ...

—W. N. P. Barbellion

Think about the last time you experienced complete pleasure—a bursting out, heart-opening uncontainable pleasure that reminds you, if only for a moment, how beautiful life can be. My guess is that it has less to do with the thrill of sensation and monetary gain but more to do with an attitude or state of awareness. Watching dolphins at play in the ocean is one of the things that does it for me. Something about their natural playfulness fills me with effervescent joy.

A youthful and enthusiastic attitude about life is key to longevity.

If we can't find pleasure in life, then it hardly seems worth putting up with all the drudgery we have to endure at times. It's not about how much money we have or our station in life. Letting go of the need to have and do more allows us the space to be awake and present to the genuine pleasure right where we are.

Learning to look at life with fresh eyes and childlike wonder can transform our lives at any age. It's not age that makes us old—it's attitude. We all have moments when we feel weary from the challenges of life, and waking up each day can, on occasion, fill us with dread and angst instead of enthusiasm. We can learn to cultivate a youthful mind and vibrant spirit at any calendar age; we just need the desire to do so. An alert flexible outlook on life also helps us to bounce back from challenges more successfully.

This morning in the *Los Angeles Times*, I read about four amazing unstoppable Southern Californians, two men and two women—ages eighty-four to ninety-four, a runner, a cyclist, a swimmer, and a triathlete—whose individual stories put a smile on my face and inspired me to do an extra mile on the treadmill. While not all of us may be motivated to pursue challenging athletic goals as they are, we can surely find inspiration in their spunk and zest for making every day count. The eighty-eight-year-old Rita Simonton, winner of five gold medals for swimming in her age group at the 2004 World Championships, says her mantra in life is "Keep busy, Keep learning," and her advice on aging comes down to "Don't dread it, revel in it."

And now in age I bud again ...

—George Herbert

Aging is often associated with stagnation and rigidity, whereas youthfulness is associated with spontaneity and flexibility. A curious and passionate love for life rejuvenates every cell in your body, and can ward off disease and decay, which makes the journey through life more pleasurable. How's that for incentive!

There is always something good and rich to savor each day if you are open to it.

Sometimes it takes a wake-up call to be able to see life anew, to recognize life for the beautiful and amazing gift that it is. My friend Meredith survived a rare type of breast cancer, met the love of her life, and now lives each day with so much gusto and joy that she looks like a completely different person than the one she was before cancer.

You can give yourself a wake-up call every morning so you can see life with fresh eyes. My personal daily wake up call is to remind myself that each day I only have the twenty-four hours right in front of me. I give thanks and remind myself that it is up to me what I make of the day.

It's up to you to cultivate new ways to enrich and celebrate your own one-of-kind life. Life isn't going to wait for us. The degree to which we enjoy life often depends on the degree to which we engage ourselves in the miracle of creation all around us. Learn to be curious about life and people. Take an interest in others. Surprise yourself and allow life to surprise you. Try on new personas and see yourself from as many fresh and unique angles as possible.

When we think life is boring and predictable, it's usually because we have become boring and predictable. When I find myself falling into a rut or routine, I make a conscious choice to stir things up a bit and try something new. I might take a new class, wear my hair different, or schedule lunch with a friend I haven't seen in a while.

Some things I am not about to change; I have no intention to eat meat after twenty-seven years, start smoking, or find a new husband. That said, sex and romance in a long-term relationship can definitely get routine, so couples have to be creative to breathe new life into their relationship. More on that later!

The earthly paradise is where I am.

—Voltaire

Joy is in the now

Instead of always planning ahead, as is my nature, I try to be more spontaneous as much as possible. Because both my husband Alan and I don't have nine-to-five jobs, we have the freedom to create our schedule as we want. Of course, it's harder when you have small children and are exhausted, and yet spending time with children is a wonderful opportunity to learn to play and be in the moment. I miss all the times when our daughter Arielle was growing up.

Sometimes I imagine going back in time and reliving different stages of her childhood together. I'm so grateful that we have much of her childhood on video, so Alan and I can watch them and reminisce any time we want. It's funny that we don't do that very often; we're too busy enjoying our time with her now. And one day hopefully I will be a grandmother and what an enchanting pleasure that will be.

Take pleasure in the ordinary things of life and learn the art of doing nothing in particular.

The thing is to be completely present at each stage of life so we can enjoy the gifts and magic that each experience offers. We are here to enjoy life and partake of all its pleasures. There are no rewards in denying yourself pleasure as far as I can tell. You don't gain points at the end of your life for all the ways you deprived yourself.

After my mum died, I found all the expensive bottles of perfume and pretty nightgowns I had given her over the years stashed away in her closet. Some she had never opened. She used to tell me she was saving them all for a special occasion, even though I frequently encouraged her to enjoy them while she could. Since then I don't save gifts until a later time, for I know that time may never come. I don't want Arielle finding a closet full of gifts I never opened after I have died.

If you can spend a perfectly useless afternoon in a perfectly useless manner, you have learned how to live.

—Lin Yutang

Give yourself permission to be amazed and in awe. The kind of pleasures I am talking about are usually free or inexpensive and don't harm you or anyone else. So indulge yourself in life; the world is filled with things for you to savor and enjoy. All you need is your active participation and appreciation.

I want to live knowing there are still some magical surprises around the corner at whatever age I happen to be at. I am not willing to settle for less than that. Are you? Discovering what's next is an adventure in itself. Give yourself the space and freedom to imagine scenarios, both reasonable and outlandish, that will open your mind to new possibilities. Who knows what might happen? If you can imagine it and dream it, anything is possible.

Engage yourself fully in your life instead of letting it pass you by. A happy life springs forth from simple, pleasure-filled moments that are right where we are. We are so conditioned to be busy and productive that we feel guilty if we take time out to rest, stare at our toes, or watch the fluffy clouds roll by.

Surely joy is the condition of life.

—Henry David Thoreau

Here are some of the things that give me pleasure and make me excited about life. Fortunately, most of these pleasures are easy, inexpensive, and good fun, with a few indulgent treats thrown in. Have fun coming up with your own joy list, and if you want to borrow from mine, be my guest.

Create your joy list

- I love wearing a pretty slinky summer dress without underwear, and I love to skinny dip on a hot summer's night. I love to walk barefoot in the sand. I would go barefoot or in sandals all year round if I could.
- Eating is one of life's greatest pleasures. I could live on Italian and Japanese food (yummy). And I adore a perfect chocolate soufflé or a warm gooey apple and berry cobbler with vanilla ice cream melting in the middle. This country has become diet obsessed, but really, is there any greater pleasure than a scrumptious satisfying meal? One of my dreams is to go to Florence and take a month long cooking class.
- Alan and Arielle are always turning me on to a vast array of eclectic music they think I would enjoy. This summer I fell in love with the music of Corrine Bailey Rae and Jack Johnson. I love to watch foreign films and eat ethnic foods. You don't have to go to India to eat great Indian food.
- I always have fresh flowers in the house whenever possible. Right now I am in love with roses in vibrant shades of fuchsia, orange, yellow, and red. Sometimes I just stand in front of a vase of the multicolored roses on my kitchen table and stare. I am quite taken aback by their sheer perfect beauty.
- I love a pile of new books at the side of my bed and the anticipation of which one to read first. Last summer I began taking beginners Italian with Arielle in preparation for her study abroad program in Italy, and this year I want to brush up on my French for a future trip to Paris.
- I love the smell of babies, pipe tobacco, fresh coffee, and Guerlain Vetyver cologne. I love lavender and lemon verbena, and I could get drunk on night blooming jasmine.
- I love the sounds of crickets in the summer, the calming cooing sound of the forest

dove, and the sound of church bells and dogs howling in unison in my neighborhood—as long as they don't go at it all night.

- I love the utter comfort of deep restorative sleep when I am exhausted after a long day of travel.
- I have been taking freeform dance classes lately and absolutely love it. I'm not exactly Isadora Duncan or Martha Graham, but when I dance I feel sexy and ageless.
- I love to stand in the grass at night, arms outstretched staring at a full silver moon, or make a picnic and lie on the beach and stare at the stars on a perfectly clear summer's night.
- I am definitely a bath person. There are shower people and bath people. My years in Japan taught me to appreciate the art of bathing. Shower and scrub first and then soak. I like to add sweet smelling oils and gels to my bath, a practice that is not allowed in Japan and only something an unknowing foreigner would do.
- There is nothing like a good foot massage done by someone who knows what they are doing, like my husband Alan for example. Now to add to that, I love a long sensual warm oil scalp massage, which makes me positively purr with pleasure.
- I love rereading old love letters and cards from Alan and Arielle. When Arielle was a child and I was mad at her for something, she would write a little note asking for my forgiveness that usually went something like this: "Dear mama so sorry I made you mad. It just popped out. Do you still love me and forgive me? Please sign yes or no in the box below. Love, from your baby Arielle." I have a treasure drawer filled with such notes.
- And of course being British, a nice cup of tea is a welcome tonic at any hour of the day. Add to that a plate of Mcvities Dark Choclolate digestive biscuits and I'm in heaven.

There is no trouble so great or grave that cannot be much diminished by a nice cup of tea.

—Bernard Paul Heroux

The magic of travel

To keep our minds youthful, we need the experience of new adventures. What better way to find adventure and stay open to chance and pleasure than when we travel. Nothing broadens our minds more than travel and seeing how people live in other parts of the world. When we experience the riches of other cultures, our own lives become richer because of it. Personally, I derive more pleasure from experience than from material things—that's why travel and food are high on my list of earthly pleasures. I would much rather have a delicious meal than a new purse, and I would choose the freedom and resources to travel over a hefty mortgage any day.

I don't love the stress of long journeys—who does?—but I do love waking up in a new foreign city. And if I'm alone, it becomes even more of an adventure. Who will I meet? What will I learn? This past fall I spent three weeks in Siena, Italy, visiting Arielle while she studied abroad. What can I say? It was my first time in Siena, and I fell in love with it. It was a memorable experience, especially sharing it with Arielle and being able to stay at her apartment. I also stayed at a bed and breakfast alone in Florence for several days. I avoided the tourist areas as much as possible and would walk for miles without any real destination in mind. I traveled by bus and train and ate where the locals ate.

> *To awaken quite alone in a strange town is one of the most*
> *pleasant sensations in the world. You are surrounded by adventure.*
>
> —Freya Stark

A chance encounter in Siena

One afternoon in bella Siena, I was sitting on a park bench waiting for Arielle to finish a class. I was writing in my journal and then looked up to see a very elegant older man sit down on the bench next to me. He was a fine, distinguished looking gentleman, dressed impeccably in a dark navy suit with a crisp white shirt and matching over coat. His tie was a burgundy stripe and matched the handkerchief in his jacket pocket. He wore a hat and tan leather gloves and carried a cane. When he took off his gloves, I noticed his neatly manicured fingers and simple gold wedding band.

For ten minutes or so he spoke to me in rapid Italian that I could barely understand except for the word *bellissima,* which he kept repeating over and over as he pointed to my face. At first I thought he was laughing at me and that perhaps I had some residue spinach stuck in my teeth from the lunch I had just devoured. But the more he kept repeating *bellissima,* I decided it couldn't be that. When I smiled and tried to explain very poorly that I don't understand Italian, I seemed to delight him even more. We both laughed and smiled at each other, and then he stood up, took my hand gently in his, bowed to me, and said very politely, *"Arriverderci, bellissima Angela."* Good-bye, beautiful Angela. And then he walked slowly away smiling to himself. I felt radiantly beautiful for days after. I can't speak for him, but for me it was a brief encounter that I will never forget.

I will always equate this sweet moment with the memory of my stay in Siena. Chance encounters like this happen all the time when we travel and take ourselves out of our everyday lives. I have met wonderful people on trains in faraway countries and had great conversations on flights, long and short. There is nothing quite like being on the road to broaden our vision of the world and even ourselves. Travel doesn't have to take you far; even

Bell' Farniente— Italian for the "beauty of doing nothing."

a trip to your next town can bring a fresh sense of adventure and lift to your spirits. Consider traveling to one new place every year at off peak times, and try and stay away from tourists. Take a train, smile at people, and talk to strangers. Trains and buses are wonderful as you get to watch the countryside go by, and at the same time start up a conversation with your fellow traveler or lose yourself in your thoughts.

The art of life is to live and to live means to be aware,
joyously, drunkenly, serenely, divinely aware.

—Henry Miller

Like many people, one of my favorite travel destinations is Hawaii. Nothing is more deliciously intoxicating than the scent of flowers after a Hawaiian rain shower. Despite growing up in damp, rainy England, I love to walk in the rain, warm rain if possible. One afternoon last year, I had a memorable experience when I was caught in a summer rainstorm on a different kind of island, the island of Manhattan, NY. The air had been muggy and the sky overcast all day. When I came out of the Whole Foods Market, the clouds burst and rain came dancing down on the empty streets.

People huddled in shop doorways waiting for the rain to pass, but I stepped out in to the warm rain dressed only in light cargo pants, a tank top, and sandals and walked the twelve blocks back to the hotel. As I walked, I passed other like-minded, carefree individuals, and we just looked and smiled at each other as we enjoyed every moment of our wet walk. I walked with my hands out stretched, hair dripping in my face, literally soaking it all in.

Laughter is good for the soul

Laugh, laugh, laugh—especially at yourself. Laughter is a sure way to keep us young at heart. It feels good to be silly and loose as opposed to tense and uptight. Laughter can relieve depression and the anxiety of aging and is a great opportunity to reconnect with our childlike goofiness. It takes wisdom to allow yourself to be foolish. Sometimes we take ourselves far too seriously.

I love to laugh till I cry, and I love it when I make someone else laugh out loud. It's exhilarating, and I wish I could do it more often. Sometimes my mum would crack herself up over the silliest thing until she literally could not stop herself laughing for several long minutes. One summer, we were out picking strawberries in a field in Yorkshire, and for no apparent reason, she burst out laughing and could not stop. Her face was smeared with juice from the red ripe strawberries, and her laughter was so infectious it made me laugh, and then my dad looked at the pair of us laughing our heads off and wondered what was going on, and he started to laugh. To witness such a lovely spontaneous eruption of joy in my mum is a memory I will cherish always.

I gave myself up so completely to present desires
and pleasures that I had no energy to waste on mere wishful thinking.

—Simone de Beauvoir

My husband is a funny guy. He can do excellent impressions of Stan Laurel, Jerry Lewis, old timers from his early days in the Catskill Mountains, and his feuding Jewish grandmas Becky and Dora. I'm not funny like that, but I do have a dry wicked sense of humor that tickles my husband and friends when they least expect it. When I get a little tipsy, I have been known to embarrass my daughter with my—how should I put it—exuberance, or loudness as she might say. I do not feel that I embarrass myself, or her, so I gently tell her to lighten up.

I find it interesting that sometimes our grown children feel self-conscious when a parent lets loose a little—as if age and being a parent should prohibit one from having fun. At a recent gathering when I was having a good time and laughing a little too loud for her liking, I had to instruct my daughter to stop being my mother.

Playing the fool

When my family and I go to the beach, Alan and Arielle love to jump in and out of waves. I, however, have a fear of being knocked down by those waves, so I usually sit and watch while they have a grand old time. Last year they begged me to join them, and tired of being the bore, I decided to go for it. I was tossed and thrown by the waves, and I got water up my nose— which I hate—sand in my hair, and I almost lost my bikini bottom. But I hadn't laughed so much in a long time.

They laughed at me because I looked so silly trying to stand up when the waves kept pushing me down. Making a fool of myself in a charming, British sort of way amuses them to no end, and I must say I love it when Arielle puts her arms around me and says, "Mom, you are so funny." Not a quality I would generally use in describing myself in the past, but I definitely enjoy living it up these days.

I must learn to love the fool in me—the one who feels too much, talks too much, takes too many
chances, wins sometimes and loses often, lacks self-control, loves and hates, hurts and gets hurt,
promises and breaks promises, laughs and cries. It alone protects me against the utterly self-
controlled tyrant whom I also harbor and who would rob me of human aliveness, humility, and
dignity but for my fool.

—Theodore I. Rubin, M.D.

Adults laugh only ten to twenty times a day, children up to three hundred to four hundred times a day. Kids laugh for no particular reason. Watch kids at play just running around playing tag or making silly faces, having the time of their lives. They laugh from the sheer joy of being alive. Adults still have that internal wellspring of joy; it's just buried under the weight of daily responsibilities and stress. A good hearty laugh feels good all over. So why don't we do it more often? When I catch myself taking myself too seriously, something I do less of as I age, I remind myself of these anonymous words of wisdom:

Blessed are we who laugh at ourselves for we shall never cease to be amused.

One way to arouse your sense of humor is to watch comedies and comedians who touch your funny bone. I love Monty Python, and it amuses me to no end that the Pythons hilariously portray my Catholic Yorkshire childhood as if it were a third world experience. My favorite comedian is Bill Maher (my fantasy dinner date). His sharp, intelligent, and opinionated wit does it for me. Stupid humor is, well, just stupid. I love politics and I love to laugh, and no one—I mean no one—combines politics, insight, and humor better than him. I wish there were more funny movies being made, but here is a partial list of some of my favorite comedies, old and new. What are your favorite comedies?

- *Some Like It Hot*
- *The Producers* (the original)
- Woody Allen's *Everything You Always Wanted to Know About Sex but Were Afraid to Ask*
- *Life of Brian*
- *The Meaning of Life*
- *The Birdcage*
- *There's Something About Mary*
- *Lost in Translation*
- *Groundhog Day*
- *Dirty Rotten Scoundrels*
- *The Wedding Crashers*
- *The 40 Year Old Virgin*
- *Little Miss Sunshine*
- *Best in Show*
- *Team America*

If you lose your sense of humor, it's just not funny anymore.

—Wavy Gravy

A little bit of what you fancy does you good

Laughter helps ease the burdens of life and is high on my list of human pleasures. You can't help but feel young when you laugh yourself silly. Still, sometimes life can get rough, and making it through a day can seem like a victory in itself. So why, I ask, are we so apt to view certain other pleasures as sinful? The word *sin* is not in my vocabulary. I'm not talking about being a pagan libertine here, but let's stop calling flourless chocolate cake or mouth-watering pasta sinful—or anything else, for that matter, that doesn't harm you or someone else. My mum always said, "a little bit of what you fancy does you good." Isn't that the truth?

I believe in rewards and treats, but I know what's good for me and what's not. I choose to see pleasure as a reward that softens the blows of life and celebrates everything else. After all, everyone is a survivor to some degree doing the best they can everyday.

Life is a mixed bag of experiences, but you decide how much pleasure and joy you allow or deprive yourself. Enjoy it all—this flawed, imperfect, beautiful, fleeting life. Cry when you need to, and even when you don't. Laugh until you cry. Find something to celebrate everyday. Pray often and have really good food and sex whenever possible. Hey, have sex, food, and laughter all at the same time if you can. Now that's a delicious treat! Ah sex, the pleasure of sex. We all want to know how to have a better sex life at any age so here we go.

Moderation with an occasional extravagant indulgence is my recipe for good living.

> *When you die, God and the angels will hold you accountable for all the pleasures you were allowed in life that you denied yourself.*
>
> —Anonymous

31

LET'S TALK ABOUT SEX

How wonderful sex can be ... Like sunshine through and through one!

—D. H. Lawrence

Great sex starts in the mind, can ward off all sorts of age-related problems, and improve your overall health. It can lower blood pressure, relieve stress, and protect your heart. Yes, sex is very good for you. It feels good and can be a lot of fun. So why is sexual pleasure so elusive for so many women, and is sex better as we get older? Well, let's see.

When a woman feels self-conscious about her body, it's hard to have great sex at any age. When you avoid certain positions, and panic if the light is on because you are worried about your tummy not being flat, or the cellulite on your hips, it's impossible to be present and open to pleasure. If you have a mental list of all the things you don't like about your body, how can you expect to enjoy much of anything, especially sex?

If you don't feel attractive, it's hard to enjoy sex. Hopefully, as we age we learn to forge a healthy connection with our body; we identify the parts we love (slim legs, pretty eyes, gorgeous hair, etc.), and we make peace with the parts we're not so enthralled with. Most men are probably not thinking about that stuff the way women are, for they're much more "in the moment." Women, on the other hand, if not worrying about our bodies, are multitasking in our minds. We're always thinking—thinking about the bills that need to be paid, what to make for tomorrow's lunch, or analytically pondering what's going on in his mind. Not exactly the kind of thoughts to arouse steamy passion, are they?

> *As a rule, when men are having sex they are usually not focused on your individual body parts, and neither should you.*

In my sex fantasy, nobody ever loves me for my mind.

—Nora Ephron

Learn to turn yourself on

There are lots of things we women can do to enhance our sexual pleasure. First is the realization that sexual pleasure is your birthright. Then you have to learn how to turn yourself on. The vagina is a muscle, and you have to use it or it can shrink and lose its elasticity. Pay a visit to *le sex shop*, and buy yourself a fancy vibrator if you are not having good sex with a partner and even if you are. Bring a girlfriend if you are shy about going solo. There are some excellent ones on the market these days (for example, Good Vibrations, Hustler, etc.).

No one is born a sex pro, so don't be self-conscious about seeking out information.

Or you could buy the tongue in cheek book *100 Of The Best Vibrators In The World* (Harper Collins) if you want a vast array to choose from. My friend Debbie said she recently went to a sex-toy party at a girlfriend's house, had a blast, and couldn't believe all the goodies out on the market. I told her to sign me up for the next party. I think it's definitely a sign of progression that we've gone from having Tupperware parties to sex-toy parties instead.

Very few women reach orgasm through intercourse alone, and many women say they can't imagine life without their little pleasure toy. Masturbation is an excellent way to practice self-reliance. Explore your own body and find out what feels good to you so you can ask your partner specifically what you want in bed. Here's where you need to be creative and assertive:

- Sometimes it's as simple as saying, *darling, why don't we try something new*. Most men will love that, whether you've been together six months or sixteen years. This is one area I can guarantee where men will enjoy being given orders and told what to do. *Take off your clothes now* or *get on top of me now* could be the most titillating words your partner could hear. I'm not talking about getting the whips and chains out, though there is nothing wrong with that if it turns you both on.
- It might mean you go out and buy a sexy video or book of erotica to share. Of the 12 billion dollar adult entertainment industry, $1 out of every $4 is spent by a woman. Or you might prefer reading about other women's fantasies in a book like Nancy Friday's *My Secret Garden*.
- Other times it may simply be you taking your partner's hand and putting it right where you want it to be, showing him the moves that feel good to you. The thing is, if you tell your partner what you want, you'll most likely get it. And if your partner is not open to giving you what you want and deserve, then you're probably with the wrong person.
- Bringing out the sex toys is not for everyone. For some couples, what's often needed to reconnect is a return to the basics—like long slow kissing and eye contact. Turn off the television and computer, and tune into each other instead.

- We moisturize our face more as we get older, so it makes sense that the vagina would need extra moisturizing too. *Lube it up, ladies!*

Too much of a good thing is wonderful.

—Mae West

Sex at any age

Sexual energy is available to us at all ages. According to a new groundbreaking study from the University of Chicago, researchers found that as we age most people keep sexually active well into their sixties, more than half have regular sex into their seventies, and between seventy-five and eighty-five, one in four people are still having regular sex. Wow, so there is more sex going on in bedrooms across America than we may have thought. But yes, sex does change when you have been making love with the same person for many years.

Some physical changes may occur as we age, but they are not necessarily negative. I certainly don't mourn the absence of my period or worrying about birth control, as it added a whole new level of freedom to my sexual expression. Menopausal women may experience vaginal dryness due to the change in hormonal levels, but this can be easily remedied with a good vaginal moisturizer such as KY Moisture Enhancing Vaginal Moisturizer.

Some menopausal women also experience a diminished libido often caused by stress, such as elderly parents, health problems, or any number of challenging life issues. The physical problems are often easier to resolve than the emotional ones. Remember, men's desires and abilities change over time too: they may have some plumbing problems and trouble sustaining an erection, or take longer to become physically aroused. Sex doesn't always have to be about penetration. Foreplay and oral sex can be the main event again like it was when we were adolescents. With love and care, these issues for both men and women can be remedied and provide opportunities for a loving couple to deepen not only their sexual intimacy, but their emotional and spiritual intimacy too.

Learning and sex till rigor mortis.

—Activist Maggie Kuhn's motto

The quest for the Big O (and I don't mean Oprah)

Then there's the quest for the Big O. While orgasms are certainly heavenly, they are not the only pleasure in sex. So seriously, ladies, when will we finally ease up with all the pressure we put on ourselves? If it's not the harsh self-criticisms about our bodies, it's the ridiculous pressure to have multiple show-stopping, earth-shattering, mind-blowing orgasms that supposedly every actress in film and television are having. Not so. While *Sex and The City* was great for women in many ways, it also left some women questioning their inability to have super-sized orgasms the way Samantha, Carrie, Charlotte, and Miranda appear to be having. On that note, couples do themselves a disservice when they start to compare their sex lives to that of others, especially to the over-the-top sex that every celebrity is seemingly having.

Yes, orgasms are powerful and healing, and to my mind one of the most sublime pleasures of life. You can't, however, make orgasms happen by trying to force them. In fact, if you are that anxious and tense, they probably won't happen at all. So relax—relax with your body, clear you mind, and enjoy the ride in more ways than one.

Enjoy all the sensory pleasures that are part of lovemaking—soft whispery kisses on the neck, his hand stroking your thigh. The worries and concerns of the world will still be there later on, but for now, practice being in the present moment and forget tomorrow's to-do list. Try keeping your eyes open and focused on your lover, and see how it intensifies your connection. Set a mood that stimulates your senses, and have fun. Create your own rituals—bathe together, light candles, sip a little red wine, and listen to music. Alan and I have music that we play only when we make love, so it has a very special meaning that is secret to us alone.

Sex doesn't have to be serious. Shared laughter can be quite an aphrodisiac and erotic too.

Mindful lovemaking is a form of meditation that brings a glow to my face like no beauty product I know of. When my skin starts to look dull, I know I need more sex. If that isn't possible, Nars makes a fabulous blusher named Orgasm. It works in a pinch but not as good as the real thing.

When I first saw a naked man I gasped with pleasure!

—Sharon Olds

Healing old wounds

For some women, sex has been mixed up with deep-rooted emotions such as shame, guilt, or anger. It may take years of counseling to release such emotions and experience the freedom of uninhibited sexual fulfillment. For many more of us, moving beyond the repressive religious and social mores that would have us believe that sex is wrong and dirty also took time to sort through and discard. I was raised Catholic in a house where my dad was embarrassed to watch kissing on TV and instantly left the room if sex came on. My mum, on the other hand, had no problem washing her naked body in front of the fire in the living room on many a winter's morn.

Once I started dating, these conflicting approaches to sex influenced me in ways I couldn't understand at the time but became clear to me years later. When I was about fifteen and waiting for a boy to come to my house to take me out on a first date, my dad did something that embarrassed me so much, it stayed with me for years after. As my date and I were about to get in the car, my dad came outside and said in a loud voice, "Angela, don't forget you're a Catholic." I didn't forget it that night or for many nights after.

The way that message played out in my head was that I became a tease. I played around with guys but wouldn't go all the way. Good Catholic girls just don't do that. And like most serious Catholic girls, I wanted to be a nun, so I had many unrequited fantasies about my local priest.

At the same time, I was always very comfortable with nudity and never had a problem whipping off my clothes, which probably made me an even bigger tease. Fortunately for me, it didn't take too long to shed that repressive Good Catholic girl label and realize that healthy sex was indeed very good for me.

Keeping the erotic alive

I speak of the erotic as the deepest life force,
a force that moves us towards living in a fundamental way.

—Audre Lorde

For long-term relationships, it definitely takes inventiveness and intention to keep sex fresh and satisfying. When love and sex are new, you're turned on before even getting to the sex. Over time, that naturally changes and sex becomes more about intimacy than fireworks. But the erotic life of a couple has to be separated from the grind and demands of daily life; otherwise it has a tendency over time to become routine and dull. For most couples, this is a tough balancing act that can be hard to do at the best of times.

Setting the intention with your partner for the possibility of a sexual interlude reaffirms the value of your erotic bond.

To keep erotic energy alive involves some planning. Part of the pleasure of sex is looking forward to it. Making a love date worked for Alan and I when Arielle was very young. One time I picked him up at the airport dressed in nothing but a trench coat and boots. We drove to a hotel where I had wine and finger foods waiting, and then we went home later that day to our everyday life. It was a sweet afternoon, and the memory of what we shared kept the sexual spark alive through other times when we could barely muster up a kiss on the cheek before we both fell into bed exhausted.

Make some stress-free time for yourselves as a couple, and make a conscious effort to show your appreciation for each other in ways that aren't necessarily sexual. Get a babysitter, go to a romantic restaurant, or book a hotel for the afternoon. It's not about planning for intercourse; it's about creating the space to reconnect sexually away from the pressures of daily life. Changing location can make a big difference for a couple. Getting away from the scene of your everyday routine, even if it's just for one night, helps eliminate distractions and brings the focus back to the two of you.

A Catch-22

Doing things together outside of the bedroom can enhance intimacy and keep you emotionally connected, even if your sex life gets temporarily stalled. Spontaneous sex is fantastic in theory, but the fact is that it's hard to maintain some degree of mystery inherent in new and adventurous sex with the inevitable predictability of a long and even deeply close relationship. Even the randiest couples have to endure an occasional dry spell. Weeks, even months, may go by without sex for some. There could be many reasons: the birth of a child, illness, or plain old everyday stress. When we disconnect sexually, we run the risk of drifting apart in more ways than just the physical. It's a bit of a catch-22 because when we don't feel emotionally close to our partner, we don't want to have sex, and the less we connect sexually, the more distant we feel emotionally. Waiting to be "in the mood" doesn't work. If you're waiting for the perfect moment, it may never appear. We have to create the mood ourselves and make it happen.

Every woman needs three husbands: one for youthful sex,
one for security as she raises her children, and one for the joyful companionship of old age.

—Margaret Mead

Longing for some mystery

Too much merging together can kill desire, even when two individuals love each other deeply. Time apart is essential if you want to keep your relationship and sex together fresh and energized. It gives us the opportunity to be missed, and so much more to share when we come back together. We can take comfort in stability and closeness without completely dousing out the sparks. We don't necessarily have to give up one to get the other. When you are together all the time and think you know your partner so well that there're no surprises, sustained desire becomes impossible.

Though Alan and I have a very deep level of closeness and connection, I don't need to know every single thing he thinks all of the time. I know his character and soul and how much he loves me, and that is everything to me. Nor do I feel a compulsion to share every last detail of my daily life and thoughts with him. It's not about being secretive, as we both love to share our thoughts and feelings; it's just that sometimes excessive talking and sharing is not always necessary for us to feel close. It allows for the possibility of surprise and the unexpected that is important to both of us. As we age, the comfort of the familiar is wonderful and reassuring, but that doesn't mean the familiar has to become old and predictable.

> *Sometimes it's not more intimacy we need, but mystery and some time apart.*

In order to keep the sizzle burning, some sex therapists suggest sharing your sexual fantasies with your partner, but I'm not sure about that. I think sexual fantasies are healthy and can add spice to one's sex life, but are perhaps best left in our own head. Just because you or your partner fantasize doesn't mean you are going to act them out. Some people look outside their relationship for sexual stimulation, but most people can't handle that, except perhaps the French.

Practice seeing your partner with fresh eyes

Time apart also affords us the ability to look at our partners with fresh eyes and see them as the world sees them—through a wider lens. I love to watch Alan with other people. I see how people, especially women, respond to his openness and ability to listen. He is also a very attractive man, and I'm sure he still notices attractive women. I hope so any way. Being married doesn't mean we become blind to the beauty of others. Or as a friend of mine noted, "Just because you're not ordering, doesn't mean you can't look at the menu." He loves women and I love that about him. And it doesn't hurt that he has a beautiful rich voice to serenade me with from time to time. Of course, some women might prefer that their partner keep their singing for the shower or the local karaoke bar. It may be endearing and for a good laugh, but might not do much for romantic sizzle.

> *Getting older does not mean that sex has to go by the wayside.*

At the end of the day, no matter how much you try and mix it up, it is still the same guy or gal. That's why sexually satisfied couples know that sometimes sex can be really good and sometimes a bit, shall we say, mediocre. Be realistic and don't panic. It doesn't mean you've fallen out of love (though sometimes it does) or that gray hair and droopy breasts mean the end of steam beneath the sheets. If that were the case, I'd be in for trouble.

A few days ago when we were making love and I was on top, I happened to look down at my breasts. To be quite honest, I didn't know whether to laugh hysterically or let out a deep mournful cry. These once full breasts of mine looked like long and lean milk jugs instead of pert and perfect champagne-glass stunners. Actually, I did laugh and then got on with what I was doing. And the fortunate thing is that Alan swears he still adores my breasts exactly the way they are—or so he tells me. He says they are still quite a handful, so I take that as a compliment.

And let's face it, if you are having sex regularly—whatever regular is for you—and it's tender, comforting, and occasionally exciting, then that's a pretty great and special thing. Sometimes the nights falling asleep and spooning with Alan in my old sweats, feet and limbs intertwined, is high on my list of earthly pleasures.

Sometimes you may need more sex, sometimes less. Sometimes we want sweet, loving sex, and sometimes we want more heat and spice. Sometimes we don't want any sex at all, and sometimes we want sex but just can't get it. Wherever you're at, know your needs and do your best to have them met one way or another.

> *The absolute yearning of one human body for another particular one …*
> *is one of life's major mysteries.*
>
> —Iris Murdoch

Resources: A Makeover for Your Mind

Books

The Fountain of Age, by Betty Friedan (Touchstone, 1993)

Not Your Mother's Midlife, by Nancy Alspaugh and Marilyn Kentz (Adrews McMeel Publishing, 2003)

If I Live to Be 100, by Neenah Ellis (Three Rivers Press, 2002)

Healthy Aging, by Andrew Weil, M.D. (Knopf, 2005)

Still Here, by Ram Dass (Riverhead Books, 2000)

The Virtues of Aging, by Jimmy Carter (Ballantine Publishing, 1998)

Another Country, by Mary Pipher, Ph.D. (Riverhead Books, 1999)

Successful Aging—The MacArthur Foundation Study, by John W. Rowe, M.D., and Robert L. Kahn, Ph.D. (Dell Trade, 1998)

From Age-ing to Sage-ing, by Zalman Schachter-Shalomi and Ronald S. Miller (Warner Books, 1995)

Grow Younger, Live Longer, by Deepak Chopra, M.D. (Three Rivers Press, 2001)

The Wisdom of Florence Scovel Shinn, by Florence Scovel Shinn (Fireside, 1989)

Ripe, by Janet Champ and Charlotte Moore (Beyond Words, 2005)

Letting Go of the Person You Used to Be, by Lama Surya Das (Broadway, 2003)

The Transformative Power of Crisis, by Robert M. Alter with Jane Alter (Regan Books, 2000)

The Noonday Demon, by Andrew Solomon (Touchstone, 2001)

When Things Fall Apart, by Pema Chodron (Shambhala, 1997)

This Thing Called You, by Ernest Holmes (Tarcher/Penguin, 1948)

It's Hard Being Human, by Angela Paul (iUniverse, 2006)

Love Your Body

BODY IMAGE

Nothing makes a woman more beautiful than the belief that she is beautiful.

—Sophia Loren

Every day we are literally bombarded with stunning images of beautiful female flesh. Millions of gorgeous young women with perfect skin, perfect breasts, and perfect thighs staring back at us from billboards, magazine covers, and even the sides of passing buses. Even if the images we are looking at happen to be of women over thirty, more often than not, those women will still appear to be pretty much near perfect. *Perfection* is a standard set by fashion magazines and movies stars that has very little to do with the majority of American women. Consider these statistics compiled by the National Eating Disorders Association:

- The average American woman is five feet four inches tall and weighs 140 pounds, yet the average American female model is five feet eleven inches tall and weighs 117 pounds.
- Most models are thinner than 98 percent of American women.

Is it any wonder that with such a smorgasbord of unattainable beauty everywhere we look, that most women are intensely critical of their looks and at best unsatisfied? According to a 2005 Dove survey conducted by Dr. Nancy Etcoff of 3,200 women ages eighteen to sixty-four in ten countries, a mere 2 percent of women consider themselves beautiful and only 9 percent feel comfortable describing themselves as attractive.

Dr. Etcoff explains that "the study shows that women are less satisfied with their beauty than with almost any other dimension of life." And don't assume that just because a woman is good looking that she doesn't go through the same harsh self-criticism. Models and actresses are famously known for their insecurities, and many stay thin through eating disorders and various chemical addictions. These apparently flawless beauties are as likely as anyone else to torture themselves with self-loathing and deprivation, and as the tabloids attest, their love affairs end in heartbreak just as often, if not more than the rest of us.

Beauty is only skin deep, but ugly goes clean to the bone.

—Dorothy Parker

Stop demeaning yourself

We have to learn to think differently and stop beating ourselves up so much. It takes vigilant determination not to let yourself get swept away in the losing game of comparing yourself to another woman, especially the actress or celebrity of the moment. It is a contest you can never win and will only leave you feeling more miserable than ever. If you sit around reading celebrity gossip magazines, will it make you happier? No, it will just push you into a downward spiral of self-disgust and judgment. No wonder most women feel bad about their looks. Isn't it time we stop buying into this demeaning nonsense? Judgment about how you're not young enough, thin enough, and drop dead gorgeous enough. Okay, you'll settle for just attractive enough.

Instead, why not start your day with five minutes of self-appreciation. Stand before a mirror and praise yourself lavishly. If you burst out laughing, that's okay. You might feel a bit foolish at first, but do it anyway. You'll get used to it eventually, and if the best comment you can come up with is *not bad,* then that's a pretty good start.

Kick the comparing habit

We all do it to some degree, and it never feels good. Let me share with you a couple examples of my own personal slip into comparing. There I was on the plane ride back to L.A., tired but exhilarated from five days in New York for the finals of the More Over 40 Model Contest. I was chosen to be a winner out of over nineteen thousand women and would soon appear on the cover of the magazine. It was quite an amazing and fortunate thing. I felt confident and yes, beautiful, and then I started to read the new *Vanity Fair* magazine I bought for the journey home.

Midway into the magazine I glanced over an article about supermodel Elle Macpherson (also apparently known in the fashion biz as The Body). The more I read about her numerous successes and brilliant life, and the more I gazed upon her ravishing body, I noticed the confidence I had been luxuriating in now drain right out of me. My life and my looks seemed oh so average next to hers. It was ridiculous but true. I had in those few moments belittled my own wonderful life by foolishly comparing it to hers.

Comparing is the single most damaging thing a woman can do to herself.

No one can make you feel inferior without your consent.

—Eleanor Roosevelt

My second example of negative comparing is one where I wasn't comparing myself to a supermodel, but to a younger version of myself. Arielle and I were featured in a mother/

daughter swimsuit story on the prime time television show, *Inside Edition*. When it aired, it was very difficult to watch myself in a swimsuit at fifty-two without comparing myself to me at say twenty-two, or even thirty-two for that matter. In fact, part of me wonders what on earth I was thinking when I agreed to do it. At the time I thought it would fun to share it with Arielle, and it was. And to be honest, I also thought I still looked pretty good in a swimsuit. In my own room or by my pool maybe, but in skimpy swimsuits I had no part in choosing and on national television, well that's another thing altogether.

So yes, at first viewing I played a running critique in my head of all my physical flaws. I thought my breasts bounced a little too much when I walked, and my thighs were not as tight as they were in my early modeling days. And yet, at a second and third viewing several hours later, I saw what I believe others saw—an attractive woman, who at fifty-two still looks pretty darn good in a swimsuit, though not one who is likely to be asked to be on the cover of *Sports Illustrated Swimsuit Issue* any time soon. The flesh-baring, bikini-wearing, younger version of me no longer exists, and I'm fine with that. I also realized that I needed to appreciate my looks as they are right now, for in another decade it will be highly unlikely that I will be asked to be on television in a swimsuit (then again, who knows).

There is an applause superior to that of the multitudes: one's own.

—Elizabeth Elton Smith

Bravo to Jamie Lee Curtis and Dove

In 2002, Jamie Lee Curtis did something that most actresses of any age would never dream of doing. The forty-three-year-old star of movies such as *Trading Places* and *Perfect* was photographed for *More* magazine in unbecoming spandex underwear and without the aid of a stylist, makeup, or flattering lighting. Looking directly in the camera with a huge friendly grin, Curtis showed the world her body exactly the way it was—a little paunch around the tummy, flab around the arms, and a tad chunky in the legs. On another page in the magazine, a picture of the sleek gorgeous "Glam Jamie" was shown. At Curtis's request, the magazine revealed that the transformation from real to glam took thirteen people and three hours. Curtis's real life photograph created quite a buzz and helped women of all ages start to feel better about their bodies.

Then last year we had new Dove Pro-Aging campaign featuring naked, fifty plus women of all shapes and sizes, smiling at the camera with all their beautiful, un-retouched imperfections. One of the women, a sparkling, white haired sixty-two-year-old grandma, was shown in her birthday suit on a giant billboard in Time Square. I was taken aback by how startling and daring, even radical, it seemed to present women in such a real and refreshing manner.

At the time, most men I spoke to about the campaign felt that all the exposed, older female flesh was a little too *in your face* for their liking. Most men, given the choice, would probably prefer to look at naked young female flesh than older. Can't fault them on that. To be honest, I prefer to look at naked young male flesh than older too. It's how we've been trained and what we're used to.

The fact is that if an older woman is going to appear naked in public, then we expect that she should at least look young, even if she isn't. Why on earth would she take her clothes off if she doesn't meet those requirements? She should represent popular culture's version of sexy and beautiful with no belly rolls, flabby arms, or cellulite, thank you very much. Just not done.

> *Wow, a campaign that actually contributes to helping a woman feel good about the way she looks. Now that's revolutionary and something to get excited about.*

We've been conditioned to believe that it's unsightly for a woman of a certain age to take off her knickers and brassiere and show herself off like that. So when I first looked at those revealing but tasteful photos, I felt excited and shocked at the same time. It was a bit like looking upon a treasure that one is not used to seeing—not something to be ashamed of, but something illusive and beautiful to smile and cheer about and has been hidden for too long. While one breakthrough photo by Curtis and the remarkable campaign from Dove won't erase the impossible ideal of how we think we should look, their unique visual statements are a huge and significant step in the right direction.

Oh Darling, let your body in, let it tie you in comfort.

—Anne Sexton

Praise yourself, gorgeous

These photos also ignited the memory of my mum stepping naked out of that makeshift bathtub in front of the fireplace in our old living room. Her confident, robust nakedness always looked beautiful to me. I felt the same way as I gazed upon these real, dazzling women in all their glory looking back at the rest of us women, as if saying, *yes, look at me, see how beautiful I am.*

Now do the same for yourself. Stand naked in front of the mirror and see how beautiful you are. Focus on the parts you like, the sensuous womanly curves, a tiny waist, or a head full of

> *If you look with the intention to see your own beauty, it will be there for you to claim and enjoy.*

beautiful curls. I look at the wrinkles around my eyes, but I also see the joy and light that shines from these eyes of mine. I look at my hands and see how thin and boney they are becoming, and yet they are lovely to me because they remind me of my mum's hands. I try and keep a sense of humor about the parts of my body that droop and the wiry hairs that are protruding in my chin. Remember—accentuate the positive and forget about the rest.

The next time you look in the mirror, just look at the way the ears rest next to the head; look at the way the hairline grows; think of all the little bones in your wrist. It is a miracle.

—Martha Graham

It's all an illusion

We know that much of what we see in Hollywood is an illusion. But nothing is more of an illusion than the fake images that are presented to us on magazine covers and beauty ads. Many hours and many tools go into perfecting one single look, not to mention the liberal airbrushing away of any slight flaw or imperfection. *More* magazine is probably the only magazine I know that generally refrains from this practice. Next time you look at the cover of a famous celebrity and lament over how you could never look like that, remember all the tricks and time that went into producing that one perfect image.

I read an article in *Vogue* where a famous supermodel stated that models these days don't even need to have great skin anymore as retouching can take care of all of that. She did say that one must still have the ideal canvas, and by that, I assume she meant great bone structure. I have seen instances, however, where noses have been slimmed, jawlines redefined, and cheeks are remade to look fuller—all by retouching.

Many of the women we see on covers and in ads are beautiful women, but in real life they are not the embodiment of perfection that is presented to us in magazines.

One actress I know remarked that she couldn't recognize herself in a beauty ad after all the airbrushing that had been done. And it is widely known that actress Kate Winslet was furious when she discovered that unbeknownst to her, several inches were digitally spliced from her torso for the cover of a women's magazine.

Further debate on this subject was sparked a few months ago when a highly retouched photo of Faith Hill appeared on the cover of *Redbook* magazine and an un-retouched version of the same photo was released on the Internet. In comparing the two, not only was her face airbrushed to line free perfection, but her already slender arms and shoulders were digitally corrected to make her appear much thinner than she really is.

For me, I am not opposed to a little discreet cleaning up of the bluish veins that pop out on the right side of my brow or the dark shadows around my eyes. I do not, however, want to erase all my lines and wrinkles and look so completely different in my pictures that when people see me in real life, they are clearly disappointed.

Use your smarts

Advertisers lure us by the promise that you too can look like the perfectly ageless woman in the beauty ads if you would just buy their new miracle cream. They stand to gain by preying on your insecurities to seduce you into buying their product. If you watch television commercials on any given night, you will be told how to lose weight, how to erase wrinkles and age spots, and how to cover gray and thinning hair.

We are all looking for the genie in a bottle of moisturizer, and there is a lot of great new technology out on the market. And yes, some cosmetic companies are finally using older models and actresses to entice us to buy their products, even though these women still appear heavily airbrushed. Many beauty products are better than ever, but as a consumer we also need to be smart and use common sense. Less wrinkles and a tighter neck in just two weeks without surgery is not going to happen, no matter how much you pay for a much hyped, new skin care discovery. The same goes for the new lip plumping glosses and lipsticks—they are expensive and don't work, so save your money.

Discontent with our changing body image as we age is a rich source of suffering for many people, and is intensified by advertisements and the pervasive notion that new things, and youthful people, are preferable to signs of wear and tear.

—Ram Dass

Cosmetic surgery is not a day at the spa

Why is it that so many women want to look like a clone of some celebrity of the moment and will go to drastic lengths to try and achieve that goal? Having cosmetic surgery is *major surgery*, my dear. Most people don't rush into it lightly, but some women are taking serious risks to get cosmetic surgery at reduced prices, and often with doctors who have no license or are not board certified. It's tragic to see women with botched face-lifts and tummy tucks who end up looking worse than before the surgery, and even put their health and life at risk. As one mom from Miami put it in a magazine interview, "I just wanted to look like a celebrity or model." Instead she has multiple scars on her stomach and thighs and is $15,000 in debt from the emergency room surgery she needed after her liposuction went seriously wrong.

I've never been particularly fond of my nose—with the wrong angle and unflattering lighting it can look too wide and portly in photos—but I've never lost sleep over it. Though I was told as a young model that I'd work more if I fixed it, I never gave it even a fleeting consideration. A cute and pert little nose just didn't seem like me. Can you imagine Barbara Streisand without her spectacular nose? Not that I'm comparing her signature olfactory to my

47

mediocre one, it's just that my nose never really bothered me despite what others may have thought.

Idol worshiping—a fad of the past

In America we have taken the cult of celebrity worship to a soulless and dangerous high. Women of all ages are getting into debt because they are rushing out to buy the latest clothes celebrities are wearing and bags they are carrying. Most of us are influenced by popular culture to some degree, but why do we give so much importance to what many generic celebrities are doing with their lives?

I think we would all be better off if we got rid of tabloids and turned off the television from time to time. That's just my vote. I won't waste money on tabloids though I do glance at them at checkout stands. Just to make sure I'm up on the important issues of the day, you know, like who in Tinseltown had a melt down or who gave birth to an alien.

Belonging to oneself—the whole essence of life lives in that.

—Ivan Turgenev

I rarely buy fashion magazines anymore, but do enjoy an occasional mind-numbing browse through the glossy pages of *Vogue* when I'm at the beauty salon. I'm a little too old for all those images of baby-faced youth, unnatural thinness, and self-indulgent fashion spreads that border on child pornography. I do love fashion, though; that's why a publication like *More* magazine is so important. It's the only hip fashion and lifestyle magazine that speaks specifically to women over forty.

Beauty and fashion can be fun and surely has its place in this serious world in which we live. The thing is to see it for what it is—entertainment and light-weight relief from the stress of life. But the more I ponder this issue of comparing, the more it seems to me almost masochistic that women allow themselves to be demeaned in this way. It's cruel and we deserve to treat ourselves better than that.

We waste too much time and money lusting for a peak into celebrity life, instead of focusing that energy and attention on staying healthy and living our own lives well.

Comparing steals away your energy and zaps your self-confidence, so why not use that energy to practice building your self-esteem up instead of tearing it down. Or at least compare yourself to someone your own age. Pay attention to how you feel about yourself after hours of looking at celebrities in magazines or on television.

Learn to have compassion for every part of your body, especially the parts you don't like. How can you possibly be satisfied with your looks and your life after time wasted on self-flagellation? So put down your whip, your *People* and *Us* magazines—with their ridiculous lists of the world's most beautiful people—and spend some time loving and appreciating the beauty that is you.

To be nobody but yourself in a world that is doing its best, night and day—to make you look like everyone else—means to fight the hardest battle which any human being can fight—and never stop fighting.

—E. E. Cummings

SELF-CARE

I have always regarded myself as the pillar of my life.

—Meryl Streep

Comparing isn't limited to only the looks department. I have found that comparing myself to anyone about anything never feels good, and certainly doesn't help me move forward in my life in any constructive way. The only exception is when I can look at another's success as a source of inspiration for how I want my life to evolve. Even then I recognize that we all have our own path and pace in life, so I use what works for me and disregard the rest. This is one of the ways I have learned to take care of myself. It takes years and experience to understand who we are and what we need, and what is best to leave alone.

You don't need permission from anyone to take care of yourself.

Self-care is a positive, nurturing act of loving kindness toward oneself. Caring for yourself is a divine expression of your belief in your true worthiness. It is a declaration that says, *I deserve to be nurtured and treated exceptionally well by others and most importantly by myself.* The problem is that many women don't feel they are worthy and deserving and give to others while neglecting themselves. Women often confuse self-care with frivolous selfishness, which it is not. Shower yourself with kindness. Take yourself out for a delicious meal; perhaps have a glass of wine and definitely a little dessert. Delight in being served, and pick up a lovely bouquet of flowers on your way home just because they make you smile. Spend time with people who appreciate you and show it through their words and actions.

Self love, my liege, is not so vile a sin as self-neglecting.

—William Shakespeare

Giving is important—it's what gives our lives meaning when we make ourselves necessary to someone else. But constantly giving to others with little thought for yourself is a sure recipe for bitterness and resentment, not to mention the physical and emotional burnout that may occur. We are wired to micromanage, even when it makes us exhausted. Multitasking may indeed be part of our female DNA, but it's up to you to make time for yourself amidst the mile-long list of tasks you feel you need to complete. Make a pledge to yourself that you will value your health as much as you value the health of your loved ones. Say it out loud, write it in your journal, or tape it on the fridge, and remember this revealing statistic:

A mom's worth equals $761,650. According to a study by Edelman Financial Services LLC, this is the salary a mom would be paid for all the work they do, from cleaning and cooking, to raising kids and social planning, as well as all that homework and family therapy we oversee along the way.

Make yourself a priority in your life

A recent online survey from the *Oprah* show revealed that a staggering 93 percent of her viewers say they have let themselves go. They put on weight, never exercised, and essentially stopped caring about their appearance. Many said they were depressed and generally felt bad about themselves, their lives, and how they looked. Some of the women felt unappreciated, and others said they felt their families took them for granted.

> *The key is to keep your mind and body active. Be good to yourself*
> *and you'll be around for a long time.*
>
> —Magdalena Skiff, 106 years old

There's one thing I know for sure: it is very rare that time for yourself is offered to you. We have to make the time and space to nurture ourselves without asking permission from anyone. Set your intention to make yourself a priority in your life, not the last on the list after everyone in your family has been taken care of.

Ask yourself in what ways have you let yourself go, and make a list of what actions you need to make to change it?

I see exhausted women running around, picking up after their families, and doing for others while they neglect themselves. Time invested in yourself is time well used. I recently saw a T-shirt with the slogan that read—*If mama ain't happy, ain't nobody happy.* Ain't that the truth.

What represents comfort to you? For me, coming home after a long day out, the first thing I do is to take off my shoes and clothes and put on my cozy gear. My Aunt Edith called it "putting on her friend." I just love that saying—putting on your friend. Mister Rogers knew what to do. He'd walk into his house, put his shoes neatly away, and change into a cozy sweater. Before I *put on my friend,* I take a relaxing bath to help me unwind from the day, and then I'll have a cup of tea and maybe a biscuit or two. I need time alone to decompress before I can be available to anyone else.

Inner nag be on her way

There is that part of ourselves that feels ugly, deformed and unacceptable. That part above all, we must learn to cherish, embrace, and call by name.

—Macrina Wiederkehr

The most important first step toward healthy self-care is to toss out the self-criticism and practice speaking kindly to yourself. It has to start there. The silent voice in your head is the one you hear all the time, so let the words be sweet and merciful. Promise yourself each morning: no self-criticism today.

Keep reminding yourself of this, and tell your inner nag to be on her way. We are genetically programmed to be flawed and imperfect—so when we can accept and relax with that we become a whole lot happier and at ease with ourselves. I have, at times in the past, been harsh with myself over what I considered to be defects in this human vessel of mine. For example, it takes me a long time to write though I am a fast reader.

Some writers can churn out book after book in the time it takes me to finish writing one. I am technologically challenged and a bit dim-witted with the computer, though I do the best I can. I am an old-fashioned kind of girl that way. I really don't enjoy sitting in front of a computer, so it's a marvel to me that I have mastered it well enough to write my books and do basic e-mailing. I complete what is mine to do, and I do it at my own pace and fashion.

Self-acceptance

I also don't do well with noise, bright lights, and too much sensory stimulation. I am not a high octane, energizer-bunny kind of person, and sometimes my constitution is more fragile than I would like it to be. This used to bother me, and I would berate myself over the fact that I couldn't match my husband's more energetic pace. I would read stories of superwomen who climbed the Himalayas or spent months roughing it out in India or the Amazon, and I would think, *God, I could never do that*. Nor in truth do I really want to.

I can do without mosquitoes, diarrhea, and a long arduous twenty-four-hour plane ride. Instead, my travel must include a hot aromatherapy bath, a king-size bed with crisp cotton sheets, and an exquisite meal at the hottest local eatery. Okay, maybe not that spiffy, but you get my drift. I challenge myself to stretch out of my comfort zone, but I also know what works for me and what doesn't. Change is good, but not when it is overly taxing and stressful.

When it comes to health, I recommend frequent doses of that rare commodity among Americans—common sense.

—Vincent Askey, M.D.

Sometimes, however, in my own private fantasy, I wish I could be like CNN International Correspondent, Christianne Amanpour, dashing around dangerous places all over the globe interviewing foreign heads of state while bombs and sirens are going off in the background. What a fascinating woman and life. I love my life, but if I could have any one else's life for a day, it would be hers.

I have learned that we are all needed in different ways, so I am not in competition with anyone. The world needs all kinds of people with all kinds of talents, abilities, and skills. Instead of asking myself, *what is wrong with me,* when something in life is difficult, I try to rephrase the question to, *what is life asking me to learn from this given experience?* It becomes more of an enquiry and not a judgment. I now see that my past perceived weaknesses are also my strengths. My need for silence and solitude has been the fertile ground for my deepening intuitiveness and self-reliance.

I also avoid comparing myself and my abilities to the way I was, say, a year ago or even yesterday as I'm changing all the time. Sometimes I have lots of energy and sometimes less. I accomplish more when I can, and relax and restore when I can't. We all need the space to do "nothing." Free time alone with no agenda or demands is as necessary to me as the air that I breathe.

I'd gone through life believing in the strength and competence of others; never in my own. Now, dazzled, I discovered that my capacities were real. It was like finding a fortune in the lining of an old coat.

—Joan Mills

Know what works for you

The next step in self-care is to identify your individual needs and take the specific steps to meet them. Ask yourself on a daily basis, *what are my needs?* Start with basic stuff like rest, food, sleep, and exercise, and then move on to the bigger things, like getting annual medical exams. It's your responsibility to yourself to be informed and proactive. Many diseases can be prevented or treated with early detection.

You can use every experience of sorrow or hardship to bring greater meaning into your life and lives of others.

Due to my dad's history with heart disease, when I turned fifty I scheduled a full exam with my cardiologist. It turned out that despite my excellent diet, I still had an elevated cholesterol count. My sister, on the other hand, had a less healthy diet and had lower cholesterol. In any family, genetics can play out in different ways. I made some slight changes to my diet, (I stopped eating egg yolks everyday and cut back on dairy) and significantly increased the amount of daily cardiovascular exercise. Because I have always been naturally thin, I was under the misguided notion that I could skimp on cardio and eat as much dairy as I wanted. Unfortunately, that's not the case. I also started taking medication, and the combination of the two helped reduce my cholesterol level quite substantially.

Be vigilant about your medical care and know your family history. Consult regularly with your primary medical doctor and gynecologist to stay on top of your midlife tune-up and individual medical requirements. At midlife, a bone density test and colon exam need to be added to your annual maintenance list.

Are your needs being met?

Then think about your emotional needs. Are the people in your life loving and supportive? If you are nervous about asking for something you want or need, go over what you want to say with a trusted friend. Most women are not very skilled at conflict resolution and shy away from confrontation. We give the cold shoulder and the silent treatment instead of dealing with our issues and emotions up front in a healthy, constructive way. Learning how to set boundaries and when to say no is essential to your emotional well-being.

It has taken me years to learn how to speak out in a clear and direct manner when I am upset and angry. I try to take a pause so I can speak from a place of truth and strength, instead of blame, and then say what needs to be said. We all feel anger, but it is a difficult emotion to deal with. We're either lashing out or forcing it in, and neither work.

Learning to express justified anger is not something women have been raised to do well. I remember as a child being admonished if I'd talk back. And then somewhere along the way, we were given the crazy message that women are supposed to sacrifice for others and suffer in silence.

In Japan, suffering in silence or the ability to endure is called *gaman suru* and is considered a noble and admirable quality, especially in women. This mindset never sat right with me—I am glad to say. When we are afraid to speak out, all that anger stays bottled up inside of us somewhere, ready to explode when we, and those around us, least expect it. That, or it shows up in our bodies as disease and mental unrest in the form of depression and neurosis.

Endurance and resilience are fine qualities in anyone, but suffering in silence at the expense of one's health and sanity is not.

If you are dealing with major challenges in life, you may need help to cope in order to make sense of the complex emotions you are experiencing. Reaching out for help when you are hurting emotionally is taking care of yourself. Get professional help if you need it. Assistance and support is available no matter what your financial status. Taking good care of oneself is a necessity, not a luxury or indulgence. So be your own best friend and most ardent supporter.

> *No one can listen to your body for you ... To grow and heal,*
> *You have to take responsibility for listening to it yourself.*
>
> —Jon Kabat-Zimm

BEAUTY TALK

There are fashion magazines and beauty books galore filled with beauty tips and advice from those in the know. By now you know this is not one of those books. I do, however, have a lifetime of tips and *tricks of the trade* that have helped me look my best.

Looking good doesn't have to be costly or take up a lot of time. Some of the most effective beauty "secrets" I swear by are inexpensive or free. Consistency is usually more important than price or fancy packaging. I am not high maintenance when it comes to beauty, but I am consistent. I would never think of going to bed without taking off my makeup, no matter how tired or inebriated I might be, and I would choose a high quality moisturizer over ultraexpensive shoes any day.

Our appearance is the first thing people notice about us before they have the opportunity to know the fabulous you on the inside. The way in which we present ourselves to the world is indicative of how we view ourselves. Unfortunately, women sometimes have the misconception that self-care equals superficial vanity. Not so. And besides, what's wrong with a little old-fashioned vanity and primping?

> *A woman's beauty is as much a part of her as her wisdom, intelligence and poise.*

My mum got her hair done every week no matter what was going on in her life. All week long she looked forward to her Saturday morning "shampoo and set," as it made her feel pampered and pretty. Even during the early stages of her dementia, she would not let people visit unless she was nicely dressed and had her false teeth in. When she could no longer take care of herself, my dad would make sure her was hair nicely combed and her moustache and chin hairs shaved before he let visitors call. He knew how important that was to her.

Appreciate your looks now

After recently looking at photos of herself from a decade ago, my friend Debbie now appreciates how hot she looked during that time. I mean, she still looks pretty darn good, but I know where she's coming from. Together we lamented our tendency to disregard our present gorgeousness by focusing instead on our perceived flaws.

Don't wait five or ten more years to look back and appreciate how beautiful you are today.

We decided to change that self-deprecating mindset by cascading ourselves with more love and appreciation right now. That way in our sixties we won't look back at photos of us today, wistfully wondering why we didn't understand how great we actually looked then.

I will not, in this lifetime anyway, be fifty-two again, so I am appreciating my life and looks while I still have the chance. You don't have to miss out on how great you look now. So strut your stuff ladies, flash your knowing confident smile, and walk with your head held high. Nothing comes close to a woman who knows who she is and how fabulous she looks.

Posture perfect

Never bend your head. Always hold it high.
Look the world straight in the eye.

—Helen Keller

Posture is high up on my list of potent and completely free beauty secrets. If you want to take years off your age and pounds off your body, learn to stand straight and tall. Your breasts will appear lifted and your tummy flatter. Shoulders back with a head held high conveys an attitude of self-respect and confidence. When we slouch and stoop, we look tired and worn out, and it actually takes more energy to slouch than it does to stand tall.

Proper posture is something we need to pay extra attention to in our midlife as our bones have a tendency to get brittle and our spines slightly bent. I have struggled with my posture for most of my life. As a child I hated being tall, so I would stoop to look like the other girls in my class.

My dad was constantly telling me to put my shoulders back and even threatened to put me in a chest brace if I kept slouching. Once I began modeling, I made a conscious effort to stand tall, but to this day it is something I am constantly checking and correcting. Here's what helps me:

- Stand as close as you can with your back against a wall. If there is a space between your lower back and the wall use your tummy muscles to try and press your lower back into the wall. This is a tough one for me, but I love it as I can actually feel my spine lengthen and adjust to its proper elongated position. Plus, it tightens the abs, which is always a bonus.

- Pilates and yoga are excellent for posture as they help strengthen the stomach and lower back, which is the trunk or core part of our bodies. Yoga helps restore the spine's natural equilibrium. Exercises like walking and running are also great.
- When sitting long hours in front of the computer, I use a firm chair with a high back. I keep my hips as far back as I can and try and avoid hunching over.
- Eat a healthy diet full of calcium to strengthen your bones and wear a good bra with proper support if you have large breasts. I can't say enough about the benefits of wearing a well-fitting bra for your overall appearance. When we wear the right bra, we get instant lift, and our clothes look better as well.

Sleep

Americans need rest but do not know it.

—Bertrand Russell

The one beauty aid that I absolutely cannot do without is sleep. In fact, I guard my sleep with my life. Some women seem to do okay with four or five hours. Not me. I definitely need a full eight hours to look good, function well, and maintain my sanity. On too little sleep, I stumble through the day as if I am in a disoriented haze of severe jet lag. In such a state, I am not very pleasant to be around.

I hate that feeling when I'm really jet lagged after crossing multiple time zones, so I am not about to put up with it when I'm not. Okay, I can handle it for a day, but anything more than that and I'm a loopy mess. Sometimes I wish I could do better on less sleep; at least then I could fit more things into my day. I could be one of those endlessly hyperproductive people that America loves so much.

But the truth is, I love to sleep and really don't want to do less of it. I love drifting off to slumberland away from the cares and concerns of life, and I love to dream. Mad, revelatory, and epic dreams that I try and remember and examine every morning. I love knowing that my subconscious mind is working out all kinds of desires and bringing me insights and inspiration that I might not otherwise grasp in my waking hours. Why would anyone trade that for a few extra hours in front of the computer or television at night?

We need more sleep, not less

I have heard it said that as we spiritually evolve, we apparently need a lot less sleep. If this is true, then I obviously have a very long way to go toward spiritual enlightenment. As much as I value meditation, I am not one to rise at 4:00 a.m. and sit for two hours meditating. Blessings to those yogis who can. I would rather sleep and then mediate when I am well rested. The comfort of deep, restorative sleep is spiritual to me—it not only allows my body rest, but it also gives my mind a necessary time-out from the stress and toil of daily life.

There is a reason we call it "beauty sleep." When we have deep, restful sleep, we not only look better—we wake feeling refreshed and full of energy. The gaunt, shadowy circles-under-the-eye look only works in Transylvania or in a teen magazine fashion spread.

To feel energized and look rejuvenated, we have to get enough of the deepest stage of sleep known as REM (rapid eye movement). In this state, our heart rate

Damage from sleep deprivation can lead to a variety of life threatening conditions according to various studies on obesity and high blood pressure.

and blood pressure is lower and the cells undergo repair—all of which is important to sustain the body's equilibrium. So why do so many women skimp on their sleep? Women who don't get enough sleep are hurting themselves in more ways than one.

Women overall have more sleep problems than men, which seems incredibly unfair when it's men's snoring that often disrupts our sleep. Okay, we women can be snorers too, or so I am told. Snoring (your own or your partner's) is one of the most common disturbers of deep sleep. So what's a gal to do when she needs her beauty sleep and the man in her life is keeping her from getting it?

Personally I'm all for reserving the right for either partner to sleep in another bedroom or couch if disruptions become unbearable. A king-sized bed also helps, or twin-sized mattresses placed side by side on a king-sized box spring. Years ago the idea of not sleeping together through the night seemed to me a sign that the romance had died, and the failure of my marriage inevitable. How silly and naïve of me. For both Alan and I, a good night's sleep has become one of the necessities in a healthy marriage. When I wake refreshed from a night of undisturbed slumber, I am a lot nicer to be around, and so is he.

Most people sleep better alone

Alan and I love to snuggle and spoon, and more often than not we fall asleep and wake up together in the same bed. Sometimes, however, when his twitching and turning overpowers my light sleeping, the most loving thing he can do for us both is to relocate to another room. If I have a wakeful night, I do the same for him. We also have different sleep patterns. I usually go to sleep earlier than him and need more sleep than he does. He can fall asleep while he's practically still brushing his teeth—like most women, it takes me a tad bit longer.

Most of us know how pregnancy and becoming a new mother can disturb our sleep, but the main culprit for many midlife women is the hormonal landmark of menopause. Hot flashes and night sweats can keep many women tossing and turning for hours. Some women find relief with lighter sheets and keeping a fan or air conditioner on at night. Personally, I hate the air conditioner at night and prefer to keep the windows open, even if it means I sweat a bit more.

We worry and multitask more than men, which makes it harder to switch off the mind when we finally lie down to sleep. It seems that most men don't have such problems when falling asleep. Usually his head's down on the pillow, a minute or two later the snoring starts, and he's well on his way to dreamland. Twenty or thirty minutes later, we are still tossing and turning, going over the day, or planning tomorrow. I have had my share of insomnia over the years and do not weather it well.

I have lost more sleep from the dread of not being able to sleep than from the lack of sleep itself. Besides the emotional and mental toil, lack of sleep clearly shows up on my face, and I am too vain for that. I also know that the inability to sleep is often psychological. The more we fear the inability to fall asleep with ease, the more anxious we become. At least I know I do. And anxiety, as we know, does not lead to restful slumber.

The main cause of insomnia: insomnia

A ruffled mind makes a restless pillow.

—Charlotte Bronte

We all have times in life that are more stressful and anxiety provoking than others. I have learned to accept that fact and relax with it. I accept that travel and jet lag will mess around with my regular sleep patterns, but I know from experience that I do adjust. I prefer to use natural remedies, but when I really need sleep and it's hard to come by, I am not opposed to using a mild sleeping pill on occasion. Like any medication of this type, taking it every day can be habit forming, so be mindful. I do not have an addictive personality, so I allow myself that freedom.

Only you know what remedy is safe and works best for you. I have no judgment around medication or natural plant relaxants when it comes to the sleep deprived and world weary. There have been moments in my life when carefully and conservatively monitored medication has pulled me through difficult times. Sometimes it is truly a matter of what gets you through the night.

Women suffer from insomnia more disproportionately than men because of our susceptibility to depression and anxiety.

Here's what works for me in the quest for a good night's sleep, and also what's best left alone:

- Regular meditation and deep abdominal breathing will help calm your mind during the day and at night.
- If you have something on your mind, write down your thoughts in a journal.
- A warm lavender-infused bath about an hour before bed will help you relax and unwind from the day. It is my signal to myself that I am preparing for sleep.
- Try and go to sleep around the same time every night and awake at the same time in the morning. Like many people, I tend to sleep longer in the winter months and rise earlier when there is more sunlight.
- Keep the bedroom dark and quiet. Use a white noise machine if there are too many distracting noises. When I go to New York, it takes me a couple days to get use to the constant noise of trucks and sirens going off all night. Alan finds that the ticking of a clock helps to put him to sleep, and both he and Arielle love eye masks. They don't work for me, and a ticking clock revs me up instead of calming me down.
- Try herbal remedies like valerian, passionflower, or melatonin.
- Eat dinner before 7:00 p.m. and avoid caffeine at night. Too much alcohol can keep you awake despite initial drowsiness. That second or third glass of wine could be the culprit. Try herbal tea or warm milk if you are not lactose intolerant.
- Don't watch the news before you go to bed unless you want nightmares. A good book helps me unwind.
- Avoid looking at the clock in the middle of the night—watching time passing by will add to your anxiety level.

Smile

Sunshine is good for your teeth.

—Anonymous

A warm open smile can make a huge difference in how we look. It's not about having perfect teeth; it's about the energy we radiate when we laugh and smile. When we smile, our inner beauty and joy light up our faces. We have no idea how lovely we look when we are animated and excited about life and happy in our own skin.

Nothing beats a beautiful genuine smile, but let's face it, yellowish coffee and nicotine stained teeth are not attractive. In California, people want to emulate movie stars, news anchors, or weather forecasters with sparkly, alabaster teeth. Blindingly white, fake looking teeth that demand the shield of sunglasses are not attractive either.

Growing up in England, it was unheard of for kids to get braces on their teeth. It was accepted that most of us had crooked teeth, and it wasn't much better in Japan either. I'd never heard of flossing until I moved to California and suffered from a serious bout of gum disease. I had braces when I was thirty because of a bad overbite and fangs that made me look like a vampire. Alan said their imperfection was charming. I did not

People in Europe do not have good teeth, and they do not seem to care. They love their espresso, wine, and cigarettes way too much.

agree. It was, however, because of the overbite that I got the braces. I must say I was thrilled with my new straight teeth and went around smiling like the village idiot for weeks. Since then I wear my retainer nightly, and sometimes I sport a night guard to avoid grinding my front teeth.

I became exemplary at oral hygiene, sometimes brushing three times a day and never failing to floss. It doesn't matter how white your teeth are if your gums are in bad shape. I tried professional whitening once, and though it looked good, I hated how it felt. Instead I use store-bought whitening kits a couple times a year, and they work perfectly fine. I actually prefer the Target kit rather than Crest White Strips, as I think they stay on better and are also less expensive.

It's best to avoid store-bought trays and gels, which can burn your gums by saturating them with too much peroxide. Strips, which restrict the chemicals to a small piece of plastic, are safer. Another teeth whitening option is taking one daily capful of 3 percent hydrogen peroxide and swishing around in your mouth for five to ten minutes.

Your mane attraction

I am not offended by all the dumb-blonde jokes because I know that I'm not dumb—I also know I'm not blonde.

—Dolly Parton

I have colored my hair for years and am not about to stop. My natural color, from what I can remember, is an unremarkable mousy medium brown. In my teens, I became a sultry, dark brunette and even experimented with fire engine red for a while. I had a perm in my twenties because I desperately wanted to look like the wild, curly-haired Maria Schneider in *Last Tango in Paris*. This was due to the fact that I was completely obsessed with the brooding, butter-loving Marlon Brando from *Last Tango* (I must have a thing about butter as you will discover later on in the chapter on faith). But I digress for a moment. Anyway I completely ruined my hair a second time due to another fantasy I had of looking like a Botticelli goddess with long, flowing waves.

I have made peace with my straight locks since then, but I can't quite imagine myself with grey hair. Some women look fabulous with grey hair while others look dowdy and old. I know a few women who have striking, platinum grey hair that looks bright and modern on them. I am not ready to be one of them yet. I love my hair blonde, beige blonde with shimmery golden highlights to be exact.

I don't buy into the notion that women over forty should not have long hair. My friends Debbie, Rone, and Pam all have a gorgeous mass of long, curly hair that looks stunning on each of them. Long or short, it's a personal choice, but know what looks good on you. Just keep it trimmed regularly and well conditioned, especially if it is long.

The most important thing is to keep you hair well cared for, no matter what color or style you choose.

As we get older, our hair needs more moisture, just like other parts of our bodies. The great thing about hair is that it always grows back, so why not experiment with a new style or color. Changing your hair is one of the easiest and immediate ways to get a new look. A few years ago, during a time of personal transition, I changed my look from long hair to a chin length bob. It was fun to try something new, but I was glad when it grew out.

As for coloring, a combination of at-home color and professional care works best for me. I cover up my grey and darker roots with L'Oreal Preference Hair Color in Medium Blonde, and then every six to eight weeks I go to my trusted colorist, Lisa Fine of the Michael Furie Salon, for highlights. If you don't want the expense of a salon treatment, home color can work just as well. I'll share with you some of my favorite pointers in maintaining your lovely locks.

- Remember to use a shade lighter than you think you need as color always comes out darker than it looks on the package.
- Long hair looks best with some longish layers to add body and texture.
- If you are a swimmer, and especially if you're a blonde, use an antichlorine shampoo to get rid of the green. I use Zerrran-Negate Hair Care products and also Splish Splash Shampoo by Circle of Friends.
- Thinning hair can happen to women as well as men and may be caused by menopause, stress, or poor nutrition. Try using a volumizing shampoo or hair restoration products like Progaine with the version formulated especially for women. Hair loss is natural—we lose about a hundred strands a day. Dramatic, sudden hair loss is different and should be checked out by a doctor.
- Wash hair every three to four days and rotate shampoos and conditioners. Over shampooing depletes the natural oils from hair and scalp. Deep condition every few weeks. If you wash everyday, use a mild shampoo such as Neutrogena Clean Replenishing or Aveda's Shampure. Both these shampoos also help to remove the chemical build up from over use of various styling products.

- Protect your hair from the sun's damaging rays with a hat or bandana, or use a sunscreen product for your hair.
- Put aside hot hair dryers and flat irons, and instead try heated rollers as they are less damaging and drying. I use Conair Instant Heating Hairsetter in the travel size.
- Highlight hair around face and hairline a shade or two lighter, as it brightens up your face and makes color look natural. Highlights work better than all-over color as there is no root regrowth and less hassle.
- To maintain a blow-dry, sleep on a silky pillowcase to avoid knots or tangles. In the morning, spritz hair with water and tame any frizz with a finishing serum like Paul Mitchell's Super Skinny Serum or Biosilk Silk Therapy.
- As you get older, steer away from dark, monochromatic colors. What worked in our twenties can look harsh and drab when we are in our fifties.
- To blend in roots in between salon visits, use Bumble and Bumble's hair powder or hair mascara by Rashell. Both these products can be found at fine beauty supply stores.
- As for those coarse and gray eyebrow hairs, avoid plucking and instead use Men Only Mustache dye. It is the only thing I have found that does the job. I use it about every two weeks or so. Don't forget to choose a lighter color, or you may end up looking like Groucho Marx as I did the first time I tried it. For medium brown brows, use the dark blonde color and leave it on for only a minute or so. You can always reapply if it's not dark enough.

Beautiful skin

*You can more powerfully influence the skin through what
you ingest than what you put on it.*

—Andrew Weil

Beautiful skin is possible for any woman at any age. The younger we start a good, basic skin-care routine, the more likely we are to have great skin in to our fifties and beyond. I watched my mum apply her trusted Nivea cream twice a day as far back as I can remember, and she had amazing clear unlined skin even in her eighties.

Hers was a typical English Rose complexion, unspoiled by sun and nourished by lots of rainy weather. Arielle has started her skin care routine early by watching me take excellent care of mine. In her teen years, it was tough to get her to be as consistent with sun protection as I would have liked. Now she's developing a career in the

Sometimes it's hard to make the connection between a gorgeous golden tan now and visible damage years later.

entertainment business where looks count (whether we like that or not), so she is fastidious about good skin care. I have always told her, "take care of your skin now, and you'll have great skin later on."

Now here's the good news—even a woman who spent years recklessly bathing in the sun can make a turnaround. We are fortunate to live at a time with such new technology and information available to us, that great skin is easier than you might think. Let's start with three basic essentials that can make a big difference:

- **Sunscreen.** If you don't liberally apply a broad spectrum high SPF sunscreen everyday, don't bother wasting your time doing anything else. The fact is that sun exposure causes up to 90 percent of skin damage-wrinkles, dark spots, and sagging. Avoid sun at peak hours if you can and always wear a wide brimmed hat. Every day I use a moisturizer like Neutrogena's Healthy Defense daily moisturizer in SPF 45, whether I am going out into the sun or not. When I go to the beach, I apply again throughout the day and use an SPF 30 on my body. In the summer months, you can catch a lot of sun just driving around in your car, so it's a good idea to keep your upper body covered in a generous amount of sunscreen.

- **Retinoids.** To rectify sun damage from the past, use a product from the family of vitamin A derivatives such as Retin-A, Tazorac, or the emollient rich formula Renova. Prescription retinoids are still considered top-of-the-line in fighting sun damage, erasing fine wrinkles, and stimulating collagen production. I have been using Renova for over ten years and prefer it over Retin-A as it is less drying for my skin. I may switch moisturizers around, but Renova is a nighttime staple I never do without. Even with less potent over-the-counter retinoid products like Neutrogena Healthy Skin Anti-Wrinkle Serum, you should still notice results after several weeks. Be aware that retinoids can make your skin extra sensitive to the sun.

- **Antioxidants.** For extra protection against the sun and added defense against environmental stress, use a moisturizer or serum brimming with antioxidants. Antioxidants fight those unhealthy, free radicals that can cause much havoc to our skin. Choose a product filled with nutrients such as soy, topical green tea, and vitamin C. I usually apply this in the morning before my tinted moisturizer and sunscreen.

Keep it simple

I tend to splurge more on skin care than I do on cosmetics, but expensive doesn't necessarily mean better. Renova is the most expensive product I use, but there are many products out there that won't burn a hole in your pocket and work just as well as the more costly brands. I keep my daily routine pretty simple. The four most important steps are to cleanse, moisturize, protect, and drink lots of water.

Here, in no particular order, is my checklist for great skin:

- Stop smoking (or best never start). Bad habits show up on your face, and this is a very bad one. Nicotine addiction is also one of the most difficult to quit.
- Don't drink through straws. Pursing lips over and over can create wrinkles, as does squinting, so invest in good quality sunglasses.
- Sleep on you back with your head elevated. Sleeping on your stomach with your face squashed into a pillow creates creases in your face and emphasizes existing wrinkles.
- Don't forget to include your neck and throat when you apply moisturizer. Use a heavier moisturizer at night than in the morning. In the winter, when my skin feels parched, I take a few drops of Burt Bee's Repair Serum or DHC's organic facial olive oil, warm it in the palm of my hand, and apply it on top of my moisturizer.
- Excessive alcohol can dehydrate the body and promote skin eruptions like Rosacea and broken blood vessels around the nose. Too much caffeine can also dehydrate skin and cause it to look saggy and sallow.
- Don't use body soap on the face. Regular perfumed soaps and grainy scrubs are too harsh for sensitive facial skin. Use a gentle cleanser that won't deter the skin of its natural oils. I've used Cetaphil for years and think it works well for most women. When I wear more makeup than usual, I use a deep cleansing oil by DHC that leaves my skin thoroughly cleansed but velvety soft.
- Avoid isopropyl alcohol-based toners, and that includes my old favorite, witch hazel. I don't know how my skin survived after using Bonne Belle facial cleanser during my twenties. I loved the squeaky clean feeling it left, but it was like using pure rubbing alcohol. Thank God I've always been big on moisturizer.
- Spritz your face throughout the day with rose or gardenia infused water. I keep a small plastic bottle of rose water in the car and always take one on flights with me. At home I keep one in the fridge so it's extra refreshing on a very hot day. It's a great way to freshen up and keeps the skin dewy and moist.
- To firm up your jaw line and melt away a double chin, try this facial workout. Look straight into a mirror, keeping shoulders relaxed. As you breathe out, stick out your chin, pushing your lower jaw and teeth forward as far as possible, and try to bite your top lip softly. Then hold for a count of five and feel your neck muscles working. If you look like a werewolf, then you're probably doing it right. Once you get the hang of it you can do it without the aid of a mirror and practice it anywhere. I do it while I'm driving (yes, I do get some funny looks) or when I'm watching television.
- Midlife skin can be sensitive, so don't use hot water, and gently pat you face dry with a towel instead of rubbing. I keep a small towel just to use on my face.
- Never go to sleep at night with makeup on, no matter how tired you are. If you are completely zonked out keep a box of moist facial wipes and a bottle of moisturizer on your bedside table for easy access.

- To soothe under eye puffiness, place two green teabags in a cup of water then place in them in the freezer for ten to fifteen minutes. Then take out the teabags, place over your closed eyes, and lie back on an elevated pillow. Relax for ten minutes, and then rinse the face and apply moisturizer. If you don't have access to tea bags use a chilled, gel-filled eye mask instead.
- To strengthen nails use a product like Barielle that was originally made for horses' hooves. Slather it on your hands at night and wear little white cotton gloves to sleep.
- For baby soft feet, use Miracle Foot Repair, Burt Bees Coconut Foot Cream, or good old Vaseline petroleum jelly. Smear it all over your feet, and then throw on a pair of old socks when you go to bed.
- To get rid of those unsightly chin hairs that sprout up around forty, use a new battery operated micro razor for women called Finishing Touch available at Bed Bath & Beyond. It very gently gets rid of any facial hair and leaves my face smooth and hair free. One caveat to keep in mind is that after frequent use of this product, the once soft facial fuzz may begin grow back thicker, so use it sparingly. You can also wax or tweeze as I have done for years. For permanent hair removal, try electrolysis.

Makeup

Since everything falls and fades, the trick is to lift and add life back to the face with the right textures and colors and use the correct techniques.

—Bobbi Brown

As I get older, I come from the less is more approach to makeup. I've had a lot of fun over the years playing with makeup and have been fortunate to work with some very talented makeup artists. These days, however, I'm more interested in makeup that helps me look healthy, fresh, and radiant. We want makeup to camouflage our flaws and bring out our natural beauty without looking like we're trying too hard.

Like most women, I love the thrill of shopping for the perfect new lipstick or glow-enhancing blush. It's wonderful how much satisfaction one can derive from such a small purchase, but the truth is that many of these products end up unused once they get home. After all, how many beige-nude lipsticks or glosses can one use (Okay, don't answer that one). I can still get a little adventurous with smoky eyes for a touch of nighttime glamour, but I leave the elaborate all-out makeup to Arielle and her friends.

With a little know how and the right tools, any woman can look gorgeous. The first step is to know the essentials and choose the right products:

- **Under-eye concealer.** As we age, the skin around the eyes starts to get thin, and dark shadows become more pronounced. Use a yellow-toned concealer that isn't too dry or greasy. A good quality concealer is as important as wearing a well-fitted bra. Apply concealer with a brush close to the lash line and the innermost corner of the eye. I also put a touch around my nose and mouth where redness can occur. To avoid creasing, finish off with a light dusting of translucent powder on top. Laura Mercier makes a fantastic concealer called Secret Camouflage. I also like Sonia Kashuk's Concealer Palette, and Bobbi Brown's creamy concealer comes in a little container with its own sheer, loose powder.

- **Foundation.** A lightweight foundation in a yellow tone looks the most natural. Stay away from heavy foundations that crack and crease as they can actually make you look older. Liquid foundations that are hydrating work well on mature skin. I prefer a low-maintenance, tinted moisturizer like Clarins Super Restorative Tinted Cream SPF 20, which comes in four very flattering shades and gives a beautiful natural glow. Sometimes, when I need a bit more coverage, I'll use a stick foundation by Bobbi Brown or MAC that also doubles as a concealer. I also love Bare Minerals Foundation, which gives great coverage but looks and feels very natural, and has an SPF 15. It is very pure, so it is also good for your skin. For extra moisture and moderate coverage, Clinique's Supermoisture Makeup is brilliant in dry winter months.

- **Powder.** Again, look for a silky powder in a lightweight, pale yellow tone. Apply it lightly to the forehead, nose, and chin. I don't use a lot of powder, just enough to blot excess oil. I prefer a little shine to a pasty look from too much powder. I like powder by MAC, The Body Shop, and Bobbi Brown. I think everyone looks better with a little color. I know I do. To get a sun kissed look without the damaging rays of the sun, use a sunless tanner. Sunless tanners have improved a lot since the early days, and you can get a really subtle natural look with many brands. Try blending a little sunless tanner in with your moisturizer, or use one of the new daily moisturizers like Jergens Natural Glow that already has sunless tanner in it. Jergens is my favorite, and I use it year round. I find it is the most natural and works great for most skin tones. If you are adding sunless tanner to a moisturizer, start with a little at first, as you can always reapply once the color develops. Be careful around the eyebrows and hairline, and be sure to include your neck. Wash you hands thoroughly afterward so you don't have telltale orange palms.

- **Final Touch.** Once your skin is "flawless," the rest of your makeup should be quick and easy, except for special events when you might want to doll it up a bit more. Always remember to blend well and use good quality makeup brushes. Sonia Kashuk for Target makes excellent and affordable brushes, as does Sephora.

I'm not saying putting on makeup will change the world or even your life, but it can be a first step in learning things about yourself you may never have discovered otherwise. At worst, you could make a big mess and have a good laugh.

—Kevyn Aucoin

This is how my basic ten minute makeup routine works:

- **Keep it natural.** In the winter, I use a rose, cream blusher applied to the middle of the apple of my cheeks and blended upward for an instant lift. In the summer, I prefer a bronzing powder in a medium golden brown that I dust over my cheeks and on the outer temples of my forehead. For lipstick, I tend toward neutral shades of beige and pink. I like matte powder eye shadow in pale neutral shades with a soft shimmer as it lasts longer. For nights out, I use a charcoal gray shadow and dark eye pencil to add definition, along with two coats of black mascara to bring out my blue eyes. It's best to avoid shadows that are glittery and too bright, especially during the day. My eyelashes are stick straight so I always use an eyelash curler.

- **For extra curl.** For extra curl, add some heat by running a Bic lighter along the rubber part of the curler for a few seconds. Test it on you hand first so you don't burn yourself. Always curl eyelashes before you put on mascara. Be gentle, and use a curler that is wide enough to cover your entire lash area. Shu Uemura makes one of the best on the market.

- **Longer lashes.** For the most definition, mascara should be applied from the base of the eyelash and then to the tip. I use the darkest black and think it works best on most women. Maybelline's Great Lash Mascara is my longtime favorite, but Arielle swears by Christian Dior's Dior Show in Blackout. Colors like blue, purple, and green only work on the young and trendy, or drag queens. To avoid looking like a raccoon, I usually avoid applying mascara to my bottom lashes. This is where I confess to a big no-no—sometimes in the summer I get my eyelashes dyed. I don't recommend it, but I must admit it does look good to have dark eyelashes when I emerge from the swimming pool.

- **Luscious lips.** I use a flesh toned lip pencil on the very edge of my lips and lots of shiny gloss to help to create the illusion of fullness. Sadly, ladies, as we age, our lips do get thinner. Fake, collagen-enhanced lips will not make you look like Angelina Jolie, but you will have cartoonish fish lips or look like The Joker, so forget it. I used to love wearing classic red lipstick but find that it doesn't look as good on my thin lips anymore. To get a similar but softer effect, I'll use a medium shade of berry or bright apricot instead. It's best to avoid darker shades as they can make thin lips look even thinner. Also, refrain from using a dark pencil around your lips unless the late 80s Elvira look floats your boat. You've heard of the "ring around the collar." Well, you don't want a "ring around the mouth."

- **Perfect brows.** Well-groomed brows with perfect arches give your face a more polished and put-together look. I love a strong brow and think it really focuses the spotlight on the eyes. Arielle has the most amazing, beautiful, and full eyebrows that make her stunning, green eyes stand out even more. In my teens, I had the overplucked, almost nonexistent brows à la Twiggy. Then in the 80s, I had very thick brows à la Margaux Hemingway; though, on a bad day, my unruly brows looked more like Sean Connery. These days, my brows are a little sparse in areas and gray and wiry in others (Men's Only Formula makes a huge difference).
- **Don't over pluck.** I avoid plucking as much as possible, apart from a few strays below the arch and in between the brows. I use Stila's Brow Set in Fair to fill in the gaps and finish off with a clear brow gel (The Body Shop makes a good one). I prefer powder rather than pencil, as I think you get a more natural look. If you are not sure about how to arch your brows or need some help in correcting overly sparse or irregular brows, visit a brow specialist at a beauty salon.

Just breathe

For breath is life, and if you breathe well you will live long on earth.

—Sanskrit Proverb

Sometimes we literally forget to breathe. When we are stressed and tense, we hold ourselves so tightly that we actually withhold the breath. Most of us are accustomed to shallow chest breathing instead of the deep abdominal breath that restores and rejuvenates every cell in the body. There are so many incredible healing benefits to breathing correctly, and you don't need to go anywhere or buy anything to do it.

All you need is awareness. Anytime, anywhere, a few moments of deep breathing can revitalize the body and calm the mind. You can practice mindful breathing sitting, lying down, standing, or even walking. Breathe through the nose, allow your abdomen and lungs to expand, and exhale slowly back out through the nose. Indian scriptures state that we are born with a certain amount of breaths, so it makes sense that the more one is able to slow down the breath, the longer we will have to live.

We take approximately seventeen thousand breaths each day—usually with little attention to the miracle that is pumping life throughout our bodies.

There is a common misconception that when we breathe in, we should simultaneously suck in the stomach and lift the chest to make our bosoms look bigger and higher. Instead, you should feel your lower abdomen and back expanding like a hot air balloon in the spirit of a seasoned opera singer, and not an anorexic model.

When I breathe from my stomach, I feel a huge difference, especially when I am stressed and tired. In fact, it takes more energy to breathe poorly from the chest than to breathe deeply from the abdomen. A few long, deep breaths improve circulation by bringing much-needed oxygen to all our vital organs. The digestion works better, and bowel elimination is more effective, which in turn improves your overall health and appearance of your skin. With so many benefits, it's no wonder our breath is considered to be the source of life. Techniques such as yoga, tai chi, or qigong combine working with the breath while engaging the body in exercise.

I took a deep breath and I listened to the old bray of my heart: I am, I am, I am.

—Sylvia Plath

Every morning in preparation for my meditation, I practice several minutes of a yogic breathing exercise that uses the technique of alternate nostril breathing. This simple technique helps calm the mind for meditation and can be used anytime during the day to alleviate stress and ward of illness. This technique works really well when I feel a cold coming on—one of the reasons it's also known as "clearing the channels." In her new book *Healthy Living from the Inside Out*, actress Mariel Hemingway describes the process in two basic steps:

First, "Raise your right hand to your face, and place your pinky and ring finger lightly on your left nostril. Hold your right nostril closed, and inhale slowly up your left nostril."

Second, "Pause and while your lungs are full of air, press the left nostril closed while lightening the pressure on the right one. Exhale slowly out your right nostril, then inhale up your right nostril, pause, and while your lungs are full of air, switch your fingers so that your right your nostril is closed again. Exhale. Do ten cycles of this breathing exercise at first, increasing length as you get comfortable."

You are what you eat

Contemporary eating habits are cause for great concern.

—Andrew Weil, M.D.

With so much information available to us on the connection between the food we eat and how well we age, it's amazing that many women still put junk in their bodies. Genetics may determine to a certain degree your basic body type and natural weight range, but you have a huge say in where you end up in that particular range. It's not about being a size two or four; it's about being healthy for your body type. There are so many delicious healthy foods available

The secrets to vibrant health and longer life are literally found right in your fridge.

to us that there is no excuse for not eating well. A diet rich in nutritional value may reduce the risk of cardiovascular diseases and provide protection against certain types of cancer.

A balanced, nutritious diet is also a great beauty aid—our hair, skin, and nails all look better when we eat healthy foods. Growing up in Yorkshire, I was a hard-core meat and potatoes gal. I loved crispy fried bacon for breakfast and couldn't get enough of Mum's shepherd's pies and Dad's Sunday roast beef dinners. In addition to bacon, weekend breakfasts consisted of fried bread, eggs, baked beans, and a strange concoction called black pudding (sheep's bloody intestines, for your information), all cooked in lard. I loved all of the above and cannot believe I am still alive. Thank God I moved to Japan! It was my eight years in Tokyo that steered me away from meat and into a healthier diet of fish, vegetables, and soy. I haven't eaten meat in twenty-seven years, and this works best for me.

Keep your portions small

I follow some basic rules and simple guidelines that help me stay healthy and energized and will hopefully ward off disease in the future. It's also a fact that caloric reduction is vital to longevity and good health, so I generally stick to smaller portions. Obesity is growing in America, and part of the problem is that portions are way too big. Just changing your dinner plate to a smaller size can make a huge difference in how much food you consume.

I'd never heard of *doggie bags* until I moved to California from Japan. My first week here in Los Angeles I had dinner at the Cheesecake Factory and could not get over how large the portions were. One entrée is big enough to feed two or three people with still enough left over for your pooch. It's no coincidence that in Japan, where the portions are small and beautifully presented, that you rarely see anyone overweight, unless you're a sumo wrestler.

Moderation is key—if you eat well most of the time you can afford those decadent treats we all crave from time to time.

People from the Japanese island of Okinawa attribute their longevity to limiting their in take of food. They adhere to the Confucian inspired adage—*Hara Hachi Bu,* meaning *eat until you are 80 percent full*. Can you imagine the majority of Americans eating only enough till they are 80 percent full? In various studies on longevity, even rats who were fed less live longer.

> *The key to a diet that will reverse the aging process is to eat foods that are both very healthy and very delicious.*
>
> —Deepak Chopra

You can learn to eat well and enjoy food without depriving yourself. Think of eating well, not in terms of deprivation, but rather in terms of nourishing yourself. When I travel to Europe and Japan, I never think about restricting what I eat, except meat that is. It's sacrilegious to refuse a tasty plate of pasta when I am in Italy, and I would never think of passing on the bread and cheese in France or the noodles that I love to slurp in Japan. The foods I eat in these countries are usually high quality and I walk a lot, so I don't feel guilty at all.

Here are some small but significant changes that can make a huge difference in how you look and feel. Keep in mind that what works for me might not work for you. For example, I am well aware of the many benefits of a raw food diet, and know several people who have been cured of serious illnesses, in large part, because they switched to a raw food way of life. Raw foods are an excellent way to heal and detoxify the body for some people.

Raw foods, however, do not work well for me. I enjoy fresh raw vegetable juices at room temperature, but a diet that consists primarily of raw foods is too harsh for my tummy to digest, no matter how long I chew the food. For the most part, I prefer lightly cooked warm foods and drinks. Even on the rare occasion when I have a cold dessert, I let it melt in my mouth first before I swallow. Know your body and what works well for your particular digestive system. Then be adventurous, keep an open mind, but don't feel guilty if you get off track—we all do—just start over again. It takes years to establish good eating habits that become second nature, so be patient with yourself and enjoy.

- I always start the day with a cup of hot water with a teaspoon of finely grated ginger and the juice of half a lemon. It will do wonders for your digestion and complexion.
- Food is not a means to an end. Take time to savor and enjoy what you eat. In France and Italy, people live to eat; in America people eat to live. Reverse this approach, and see eating well as a sensory experience to be relished.
- Eat only when hungry, and know when to stop. Smaller meals eaten more often increase your energy level and are easier to digest.
- Eat only 100 percent whole grain breads and cereals. Eat plenty of live, wholesome, and colorful foods that oxygenate your body. Think of the gorgeous colors of nature and say good-bye to processed foods, white flour, and sugar that have no nutritional value at all. Buy organic produce whenever possible.
- Don't skip breakfast. A healthy breakfast provides energy for the day ahead, and you will be less likely to indulge in unhealthy cravings.
- Don't stock unhealthy foods at home. If you don't have them around, you can't eat them.
- Make lunch your main meal of the day, and eat light in the evening like the Italians do. It's easier on your digestive system, and heavy dinners make it harder to lose weight as your metabolism slows down at night.
- To limit nighttime eating, give yourself a cutoff time of at least three to four hours before you go to sleep. I brush and floss my teeth around 8:00 p.m., and try not to eat a morsel of food after that. Of course, there'll always be exceptions, but the hassle of having to brush and floss a second time usually helps me adhere to this rule.

- Avoid the artificial sweetener aspartame, better known to many as NutraSweet and Equal. Diet colas are loaded with this. Try other, safer sweeteners like Splenda or the herb stevia instead. I prefer a little honey in my tea and a touch of organic grade B maple syrup on my oatmeal. And if I'm going to have sugar, I eat the real thing but keep it minimal.
- Never let yourself get hungry to the point of starving. Missing meals are a guarantee to send your energy levels crashing. Keep some healthy energy snacks on hand, such as celery and raw almond butter, dried fruit, and a handful of raw unsalted nuts.
- Avoid fat-free products. Fat free means more sugar and more calories.
- Grill, steam, roast, or bake. Do not fry your food.
- Eat fish at least twice a week to boost your heart health and keep your skin looking youthful. Fatty fish like salmon and sardines are high in omega-3 fatty acids and can reduce the risk of heart disease and fend of depression. I also take an omega-3 supplement every day.
- Fruit can cause indigestion when eaten with other foods, so it is best eaten alone. I make an exception with a fresh fruit pie or cobbler.
- Avoid saturated fats from animal and heavy dairy products that give us high cholesterol. Eat polyunsaturated fats and monounsaturated fats found in avocadoes, olive oil (extra virgin of course), and nuts.
- Always bring your own food when you fly. Microwaved airline food is disgusting and dead. Do not eat it. Often I'll bring two or three bottles of organic unsweetened baby food. It's a quick and easy way to get a nutritious snack, and there are so many delicious options. I like the apple, plum, oatmeal combo or banana, apples, and pears. Whole Foods sells the Organic Baby products, which are my favorite.
- For a healthy alternative to the ghastly Ensure beverage, try Eden Blend Rice and Soy Beverage. It's a delicious and satisfying way to get extra nourishment during or recovering from an illness. I drink it anytime and make sure to carry a few single sized cartons when I travel.
- Stay clear of all-you-can-eat buffets unless you have enormous self-discipline. With so much variety, it's hard to not over indulge.
- If you eat eggs, meat, and poultry, be sure to choose organic produce that are free from antibiotics and hormones. The same goes for milk.
- Be aware of your trigger points that create emotional eating. When you are stressed or depressed, many people reach for comfort foods. While heavy starches and sugar-laden treats may soothe you in the short term, you will probably feel lousy when you hit the scales later on. Try exercise or low-cal complex carbohydrates to give you a quick mood boost. Reward or de-stress yourself with a nonfood reward like a massage or a heart-to-heart with a good friend instead.

A 101 of super power foods

Here's my list of power foods that I try and include into my diet everyday. I keep tabs on how much fruit and vegetables I eat each day, and make sure I am getting enough protein and calcium in my diet.

- Avocados, asparagus, and broccoli
- Blueberries, melons, and apples
- Collard greens, spinach, and kale
- Salmon, sardines, and soy
- Oatmeal, yogurt, cashews, and almonds
- Tomatoes, yams, and carrots
- Egg whites, sea-kelp, and beans
- Brown rice, whole-grain breads, crackers, and pastas
- Raw goat milk and cheese and feta
- Wheat grass juice, prunes, ginger, and lemons

These are some of my daily favorite meals that use all of the ingredients listed above.

Breakfast:

Most days I eat Irish oatmeal with a little soy or goat's milk, blueberries, and a touch of maple syrup or cinnamon sprinkled on top. For a more substantial breakfast, I love a high protein egg white-scramble made with scallions, tomatoes, and grated goat cheese or feta with a side of whole grain toast. Sometimes I might add some wild smoked salmon to it for extra protein. I like to spread raw almond butter on my toast and a touch of unsweetened apricot jam. If I am rushed in a morning or not getting enough greens, I drink a powdered green foods supplement loaded with really good stuff, mixed with soy milk and banana. My favorite green drink brand is called Green Vibrancy and is available at most health food stores.

Lunch:

If I'm at home, I make brown rice, steamed green vegetables, hijiki (a type of sea kelp), and grilled tofu marinated in ginger and low sodium soy sauce—or perhaps, brown rice and curried yellow lentils with a cooling cucumber salad on the side. I also enjoy a soy tempeh or veggie burger on a whole-wheat bun, alfalfa sprouts, and tomato (I usually only eat half of the bun, but I do love bread). A good stand by for me, if I have to eat on the go, is a tuna avocado sushi roll made with brown rice from my local health food store. I also love all kinds of vegetable soups, any time of year, and heartier stews in the winter. I can make a meal out of soup and a crispy chunk of whole grain bread.

I love pasta, but at home I use whole grain pasta mixed with garlic, broccoli, tomatoes, basil, olive oil, sea salt, cracked black pepper, and a touch of fresh grated Parmesan cheese.

When I eat out in a really fine Italian restaurant, however, I eat the real thing but pass on heavy cream sauces.

Snacks:

A mid-afternoon pick-me-up might be a one ounce shot of wheat grass, carrot, celery, and beet juice or my Green Vibrancy drink blended with a banana. I also like Finn Crisp rye crackers with a little tomato, basil, and hummus, or a few slices of apple and a small piece of goat's cheese. Sometimes I eat a few sardines straight from the can or a handful of edamame (soybeans in the shell).

Dinner:

I like to make a spinach salad with avocado, cooked egg whites, poached or grilled wild salmon, garbanzo beans, asparagus, and beets, tossed with olive oil, lemon, and balsamic vinegar. Another choice might be tofu and daikon radish simmered in a comforting bowl of miso soup. Sometimes I'll have oatmeal for dinner if I want to eat very light.

Desserts and treats:

I love chocolate, so I'm thrilled to know that dark chocolate in small amounts is known to be good for the heart and blood vessels. Another way I satisfy my sweet tooth is with low fat Greek yogurt topped with a sprinkle of cinnamon or organic applesauce. A scoop of soy ice cream and an oatmeal raisin or ginger cookie is another favorite. A baked yam or apple with a small dab of raw butter and sprinkling of maple syrup on top is another nutritious and filling dessert.

Beverages:

- My main beverage is unchilled water with a squeeze of lemon. I drink this frequently throughout the day, and I add a few slices of cucumber or mint for variety. I never touch carbonated sodas, and I only drink herbal teas like ginger, mint, and chamomile sweetened with a touch of honey. Recently, I have been enjoying Bengal Spice by Celestial Seasonings with a little soy milk. I usually don't drink fruit juice, but if do, I will dilute it with water so it's not too sweet. I drink green tea on occasion (I practically lived on it during my years in Japan) for the powerful antioxidants that protect against heart disease, high cholesterol, and high blood pressure—to name just a few of it's healing benefits.

- I rarely drink alcohol apart from an occasional glass of red wine or cocktail when I go out for dinner. I limit myself to one cappuccino or soy latte a day. A delicious and satisfying alternative to regular coffee is a product called Teeccino—mocha flavor. Teeccino is a caffeine-free blend of herbs, nuts, and fruits that are roasted and ground to brew and taste like coffee—well to coffee novices like me. If you need the morning crank of the real thing, try limiting it to one or two a day. Too much caffeine can give you the jitters and can deplete the immune system, so try replacing your second coffee with herbal or green tea to boost your metabolism.

In general, mankind, since the improvement of cookery,
eats twice as much as nature requires.

—Benjamin Franklin

International fare

Variety is the spice of life, especially when it comes to food. So here, in no particular order, are some of my favorite foods from around the world:

- **Mediterranean.** The ancient Greeks knew a thing two on how to live and eat well. So follow a Mediterranean diet—high in fruit, vegetables, whole grains, fish, and olive oil topped off with a glass or two of red wine—and you can't go wrong. Add some feta cheese, couscous, olives, hummus, and chickpeas to a salad and you a have a delicious, nutritious meal.

- **Japanese.** A typical Japanese diet rich in soy, fish, and sea vegetables is the foundation of my healthy eating lifestyle. Women in Japan, and especially on the island of Okinawa, have substantially less osteoporosis than women in America. The reason: a daily diet of soy, fish, and green tea. I have had little to no menopausal symptoms, but according to my gynecologist Dr. Renee Cotter, I am in the rare 3 percent of American women. I'm sure my thirty plus years of a diet rich in soy and fish is a huge factor in that. You can add more soy to your diet by eating edamame, miso soup, or choose from the vast array of soy burgers available at most markets. Try soy milk and soy ice cream for more calcium instead of the usual dairy versions. A soy latte with a pinch of dark chocolate powder on top is another treat I allow myself now and again.

- **Italian.** I love to eat great pasta and do so frequently, especially when I travel. I stick with lighter olive oil based fare and stay way from dishes that are heavy and rich. There are so many great options with Italian cuisine: wonderful seafood and vegetarian antipasto, grilled fish, and yummy soups.

- **Indian.** Ah, and Indian cuisine. Growing up in England, I experienced wonderful Indian food from an early age. I still love Indian food, but long ago passed on the Chicken Tikka Masala, in favor of the many vegetarian dishes that are in abundance in Indian cuisine. Lentils, chickpeas, spinach, and eggplant curries are my favorites. I prefer southern Indian vegetarian food that is lightly spiced and not cooked in heavy ghee, which is clarified butter.

Rx for tummy troubles

According to Ayurveda, the five-thousand-year-old Indian healing system, good digestion is the foundation to overall health. I know from experience that when my digestion isn't working correctly, every organ in my system feels out of balance. My skin and hair look dull, and excessive bloating means I can't fit into my clothes.

How you eat is just as important as what you eat. We all have areas in our bodies where we carry stress. Some people get headaches and backaches; others, like me, carry stress and tension in their stomachs. When I feel troubled or some emotion is not "digesting" well, I get knots in my tummy. I know my body well enough to understand that I need to pay attention to what my "gut" is trying to tell me.

Like many women, I have on occasion suffered from mild IBS (irritable bowel syndrome). Because of this, I have spent a lot of time researching and experimenting with different remedies. Chronic, excessive gas and belching don't feel good and are not pleasant to be around. Digestive health is very important to me and should be to you. As we age, our digestive systems become more sluggish and have to work a lot harder. That big cheeseburger that seemed to go down okay in your twenties may not sit well in your tummy at midlife. As gastro-savvy as I am, I still endure occasional bouts of digestive malaise. Here's what I have learned and what works for me.

- Squeeze the juice from half a lemon into warm water and drink twenty minutes before eating to stimulate digestion. Lemon is one of the most powerful foods for supporting the digestive organs.
- Use a good digestive plant enzyme before you eat. You can find excellent ones like Garden of Life at most health food stores. I keep some at home and in my purse.
- Do not drink while you eat as it prohibits proper digestion and neutralizes the benefits of the enzymes you have just taken.
- Chew, chew, and chew some more. Do not gobble up your food. We speed through a meal like we speed through life. We're ready to shovel in the next fork load of food before we've finished eating the food that's already in our mouths. What's that all about? Chew your food until it is liquefied—only then can it be properly digested. I constantly have to remind myself of this, just as I have to in regards to my posture and correct breathing.
- Practice mindful eating. Multitasking while you eat is a sure fire way to overeat and get indigestion. I confess that I do enjoy watching television while I eat sometimes. If you are feeling highly emotional or agitated, your food will not digest well, so it is best not to eat much at such times. Try a small bowl of soup or oatmeal instead.

- Leftover food is best left alone. Eat only fresh food, freshly prepared. I won't eat anything that has been cooked and then left in the fridge overnight.
- According to the Ayurvedic system, eating warm foods and hot drinks whenever possible strengthens your *Agni,* or digestive fire. Add warming spices such as ginger, tumeric, and cayenne to your food. Ginger is a wonder spice known to ease nausea and reduce inflammation.
- To aid digestion after a meal, slowly sip a warm cup of herbal tea such as peppermint or lemon-ginger. I also enjoy Stomach Ease Tea by Yogi Tea Company.
- Use acidophilus with a high live probiotic content to promote healthy intestinal bacteria. Bio K is an amazing product with over fifty billion live bacteria. It's expensive, so I buy a pack that contains six small individual drinks and use it one week a month. It comes in plain, fruity, or nondairy. It's especially beneficial after a course of antibiotics or intense tummy upset to restore healthy bacteria in your gut.
- Acupuncture and acupressure help me a lot when I am going through a rough bout of tummy distress. For do-it-yourself acupressure, press on the web of your hand between the index finger and thumb. Try this on both hands to help stimulate the large intestine.
- Aloe Vera juice in an herbal stomach formula containing peppermint leaf, ginger root, slippery-elm leaf, and fennel seed helps soothe and settle a distraught tummy.
- To neutralize an over acidic stomach, add one teaspoon of baking soda to a large class of water.
- When all else fails, use a heating pad or old-fashioned water bottle to soothe tummy woes.

Time to detox

Sometimes, despite our best intentions, we all get off track with our diet and overindulge once in a while. For many people, it happens during the end of the year holiday season. For others, their good eating habits slip, and they gain a few extra pounds when they are away on vacation. When I return from a holiday in Europe, I usually go on a simple detox for a few days to clean out my system and give my digestion a well needed rest.

Even though I basically eat good food while I'm away, I still consume more sugar, alcohol, and carbohydrates than I normally do at home. I do this mini detox on occasion throughout the year and always feel rejuvenated and lighter afterward. You don't have to go to a spa to detox; you can do it right in your home. Here are a few guidelines to help you get started:

- A simple detox involves drinking lots of water, eating only natural fresh organic produce, eliminating dairy products, all animal products, processed foods, sugar, caffeine, and of course, alcohol. Do this for five to seven days, and you will notice a huge difference in how you look and feel.

- For a more intensive detox, you could try a juice fast for a few days. If you haven't fasted before, it's best to work with an experienced nutritionist or health practitioner to guide you through it. I like to fast for a day about once a month.

- I eat very light—mostly oatmeal, miso, or veggie soup—when I am I ill and my body needs healing. I start the day with my usual lemon juice, ginger, and water. I add to that a pinch of cayenne and half a teaspoon of grade B organic maple syrup to help cleanse and aid circulation. Sometimes I will drink only this for a twenty-four hour fast, and I know people who do very well on this for several days.

- If you eat well in general, then you don't have the same amount of toxins or waste that a person who smokes and eats lots of processed foods does. Long fasts can work miracles on people who have lived a very toxic lifestyle. But it's still debatable amongst many health practitioners on the benefits of extensive fasting for the rest of us.

- Some people swear by enemas and colonics, but they are not my cup of tea. I tried a colonic once. Actually, it was a his/her experience that I shared with my husband (what were we thinking?). It was so intensely uncomfortable I vowed I would never do it again. I also stay away from laxatives. I had one very nasty laxative nightmare—I will spare you the details—except to say that I spent several hours on my bedroom floor with acute abdominal cramps and internal damage that plagued me for weeks after. To stimulate regular bowel elimination, eat a diet rich in natural fiber instead. I drink pure 100 percent organic prune juice and get good results from a gentle herbal supplement called Cascara Sagrada and Smooth Move tea by Traditional Medicinals.

MOVE YOUR BODY

There are so many excellent reasons to exercise, and they go far beyond looking good and losing weight. For starters, it makes you feel good and wards of depression. I love the way I feel after I've worked up a good sweat at the gym. All those endorphins that get stimulated from a great cardiovascular workout lift my mood and calm my nervous system. If I am feeling stressed and anxious, a good brisk walk always makes me feel better.

It's just not possible to be healthy and lead a sedentary life style. There's no way around that, and no excuse. Everyone can walk or dance around the living room, even if you can't afford to join a gym. The hard fact is the older we get, the more important exercise becomes. It's best to do some form of exercise every day, but even three times a week can make a huge difference in how you look and feel.

To have a strong fit body you have to eat less and exercise regularly.

I like the shape of muscle, and I like to have the muscle to move with power in the world.

—Joanna Frueh

When we reach midlife, our metabolism slows down, so we need more cardiovascular exercise to keep weight off. We also need to pay extra attention to maintaining healthy bones and muscle mass through weight-bearing exercise. Regular exercise also helps prevent heart disease and is good for the lungs too. So with all these benefits that stave off many of the negative effects of aging, it's time to break a sweat and get off the couch. Your health and ultimately your life depend on it.

A serious commitment to daily exercise can add years to your life and keep you more fit than ever. Aging does not mean that your body has to atrophy or decay, but if you don't get moving, that's what happens. No one can exercise for you—it's up to you—so no more excuses. Stop waiting to be in the mood for exercise, and just do it.

- A balance of stretching, toning, and cardiovascular is important for midlife health. I like a combination of yoga, treadmill, and light weights.

- Exercise in the morning if possible for more energy throughout the day.
- Find ways to incorporate exercise into your life everyday. Walk on your lunch break, take the stairs instead of the escalator, and park your car further away from the store. Think incline and climb anytime you can.
- Make exercise a social thing. Go bike riding by the beach with friends or schedule a weekend hike with a girlfriend to catch up. Long summer days mean you can take advantage of the extra sunlight to walk or run outside.
- When you travel, take a skip rope with you. Jumping rope is a great cardiovascular exercise and tones the arms and legs as well. You can do it anywhere, anytime.
- Add variety so you don't get bored. I like to swim in the summer and want to try Pilates, tai chi, and salsa dancing.
- Energetic sex is a great cardiovascular workout.

MENOPAUSE

After working with thousands of women who have gone through this process, as well as experiencing it myself, I can say with great assurance that menopause is an exciting developmental stage—one that, when participated in consciously, holds enormous promise for transforming and healing our bodies, minds, and spirits at the deepest levels.

—Christiane Northrup, M.D.

I'm no expert on the challenges of menopause, but I do believe that many of the things I have already talked about can make a difference in how you experience and deal with the "change." I was not aware at the time that many of the natural habits I had made a part of my life all those years ago would aid in my experience of menopause today. Daily meditation, regular exercise, and a healthy nutritious diet rich in soy are a few. You may need to talk to your gynecologist about options to deal with the physical and emotional changes you are experiencing with menopause. We all experience it in various ways and degrees. There's no one way to deal with menopause, and it may take time to figure out what works best for you. There are lots of things you can do to ease you discomfort and angst, but you have to be proactive and try different things.

For most women menopause is a gradual process rather than an overnight event.

Many women struggle through a whole gamut of harsh menopausal symptoms that keep them up at night and tired and moody during the day. As estrogen production slowly decreases, you may experience hot flashes, irregular periods, and unpredictable mood swings that leave you teary eyed at the smallest thing. My sister Sharon hasn't had a period in over five months, but wishes the premenstrual-like symptoms she and her family endure every month would disappear along with it. Her daughter Olivia just started her period, so with two females going through hormonal hell in one house, my nephew and brother-in-law are trying their best to stay out of harm's way.

I may have been spared many of the challenges of menopause, but I've had my share of female "troubles." In my late forties, it was discovered after years of heavy bleeding that I had a severe case of endometriosis. In endometriosis, for some mysterious reason, the tissue that normally forms the lining of the uterus grows in other areas of the pelvis and sometimes outside the pelvis as well.

It was hard to detect because I did not have the pelvic pain or discomfort during sexual intercourse that often accompanies endometriosis. But I was anemic and exhausted from periods that sometimes lasted two weeks. A high dose shot of progesterone administered every three months eased this condition and completely stopped my periods. Progesterone in the form of Depo Provera allows the endometriosis to regress by making a woman temporarily menopausal.

I was absolutely thrilled to have no more periods and relieved that I felt well and full of energy again. I didn't even mind the extra weight that I put on that was one of the side effects of the medication. I stayed on this

Perception and perspective, like much of what we experience in life, will have a significant affect on how you deal with menopause.

treatment for about five years until a routine blood test showed that I was clearly in the midst of the real thing—menopause. I no longer needed to be on progesterone because menopause decreases hormone levels and the disease becomes inactive.

I did experience some occasional insomnia, but I was also dealing with my mum's declining health, my dad's heart surgery, and Arielle going away to college. The fact is, I had a lot of things on my mind that kept me up worried at night, so I have no idea if or how much menopause contributed to my many restless nights. I never experienced night sweats or hot flashes, but I was often emotional and teary eyed—who wouldn't be, going through all those life-changing events at one time.

Menopause is another transition in life that has the potential to be a positive experience if we choose to think of it that way. Yes, it can be annoying at best and sometimes downright awful. But it is not a disease as we have falsely been led to believe. If you think of it that way, it will only add to your misery. Go beyond the outdated notions that menopause means the end of your femininity, allure, and sex appeal. The end of your menstrual periods is the beginning of a new crossroad and opportunity for personal reinvention. Heed the wisdom of your all-knowing inner goddess and discard any false beliefs that limit you from living your life to its fabulous fullest.

Menopause is a time to pay extra attention to yourself. Listen to your body and your emotions, and give yourself the supreme care that is being asked of you. Let go of that which no longer serves you, and invite that which is trying to emerge. An end always has a beginning, and today's midlife woman has many of those still ahead.

I am a testament that it is possible to take on this passage in life and embrace it. I will tell you that you do not have to take this transition lying down. You have choices! You have options! You have solutions!

—Suzanne Somers

FASHION FORWARD 101

Balls are to men what purses are to women.

—Carrie—*Sex and the City*

I love fashion and dressing up and think it's one of the many joys of being a woman. When I am entrenched in writing, I sit in front of the computer wearing old sweatpants or an oversized schmata for days on end. Comfort is my priority during this time, and I am not thinking about how I look. But when I get the chance to go out on the town or travel to New York, Japan, or Europe, I thoroughly enjoy putting on my "face" and looking glamorous. Tokyo is the most stylish city in the world, and many of its women and men take fashion very seriously.

The Italians, French, and New Yorkers may be known for their chic style, but in Tokyo, fashion is elevated to an art form. I got to wear some stunning designer gowns during my modeling years, as well as some weird and wacky outfits by up and coming young Japanese designers.

Over the years I have learned which styles suit me best and which to avoid. It's fun to experiment, but also to know which silhouettes and styles flatter your shape and body. It's best to avoid fads and anything overly trendy. You can be stylish and modern without looking like a fashion victim. As we age and our bodies change, what looked good in our younger years may no longer look appropriate.

Great style is timeless, ageless, and doesn't have to burn holes in your pockets either.

I used to wear lots of short skirts, but now I prefer to keep the hemline an inch or so above my knee instead. I still like short, just not as short as what worked in my twenties or thirties. It is more becoming and age appropriate, even if you have great legs. Some midlife women are no longer comfortable showing their bare arms so they cover up more—others are self-conscious about their necks and can't wait for cooler weather to come around so they can bring out the turtlenecks.

I know women with great individual style who look amazing in outfits that wouldn't work well for me. A friend of mine is into beautiful colorful scarves and uses them in wonderfully imaginative ways. Another friend wears unique oversized pieces of jewelry with great panache.

For me, simple and classic with a touch of sexy and glamorous works best. I stick with neutral colors, especially in winter. I love navy, gray, and black with the occasional red, yellow, cobalt blue, or purple.

Fashion fades, only style remains the same.

—Coco Chanel

Style not price

I don't spend a lot of money on clothes. I might buy a few quality key pieces each season and supplement with inexpensive items like T-shirts and tank tops from Target, Old Navy, or the Gap. It doesn't make sense to me to pay $50 for a T-shirt when I can basically get the same thing at Target for $10. I'd rather put that money toward a new handbag or cashmere shawl as a treat when I'm in Europe. I've bought several items from Isaac Mizrahi's chic and inexpensive collection available at Target. Who doesn't love a great bargain? I keep my eye on coveted items and wait for special sale events to earn discounts.

Preseason sales are a good time to shop, as are after Christmas and end of summer sales.

Last winter, I kept my eye on cashmere sweaters at Bloomingdale's and Banana Republic, but instead of buying them at full price at the peak of the season, I waited till they were on sale at 50 percent off during the January sales. Sometimes Arielle and I will rummage through the racks at the inexpensive designer knock-off stores like Forever 21, H&M, and Mango. Most of the stuff is way too trendy for me, but on occasion I do get some decent tops from these stores.

The scrunchie story

I've passed on to Arielle many of the dresses I no longer wear, and now she wears them with her own unique flair. I love how she can wear something I once wore and make it look completely new and fresh. I am her main supplier of vintage pieces. I frequently ask her opinion on what to wear, and on occasion she gives me her unsolicited opinion whether I want it or not. Last year when I visited her in Siena, Italy, I committed a fashion faux pas of gigantic proportion that she hasn't let me forget since. We laugh about it now, but at the time she was deadly serious.

We were sitting on the steps of a church in a crowded piazza eating delicious Panini sandwiches. I was absorbed in my sandwich and people watching when Arielle pointed out, quite aghast, that I was wearing an old, blue scrunchie in my hair. I had neglected to replace the scrunchie with a black elastic band when we departed the hotel that morning.

She turned to me and in the spirit of her idol, Carrie Bradshaw, exclaimed, "Mom! I can't believe you are wearing a scrunchie in public, in Italy of all places!" Well of course, I knew that wearing a scrunchie anywhere but at home was a fashion no-no, but hey, I slipped up. It happens to the best of us.

Over the years I have learned that what is important
in a dress is the woman who is wearing it.

—Yves Saint Laurent

Here is my short list of midlife fashion do's and don'ts (Some of these apply at any age):

- Do not wear scrunchies in public. Use a black elastic band or tortoiseshell hair clip instead.
- Do not reveal your abdomen no matter how many crunches you do. Revealing excessive flesh is cheesy not sexy. When in doubt, cover up. If you want to show a little cleavage, refrain from showing too much leg.
- Black is always classic. You can never have too many simple, little black cocktail dresses to dress up or down.
- Super low-rise jeans with bright colored or leopard thongs peeping out look cheap and tacky at any age.
- A crisp white shirt, pearls, or diamonds (fake works just as well) will brighten up your face.
- Invest in high quality undergarments. A seamless bra like Barely There in nude works best under T-shirts and knit fabrics. To eliminate the appearance of bulges and bumps, try a body smoother garment that works like a corset. The new ones are lot more comfortable than the old-fashioned kinds our mothers used to wear. Spanx and Donna Karan make good ones.
- Throw away shabby clothes that make you look like a bag lady. Comfortable doesn't mean unkempt and slovenly when you are out in public (you can get away with anything at home). I recycle some clothes that are in decent condition and hold on to expensive pieces that will most likely come back in fashion.
- Use accessories to add a fun pop of color to a neutral toned outfit—a scarf, bright leather gloves, chunky men's vintage watch, shoes, or a handbag, perhaps.
- A medium heeled, sling-back stiletto in black or dark brown faux crocodile makes any leg look slimmer. A pencil skirt and stiletto heels are sexy and classic. I am not a big fan of flat shoes apart from ballerina slippers, Converse sneakers, or flip-flops in

the summer. Ballerina slippers and horse riding boots look best on slim legs and small calves.

- Choose quality fabrics like cashmere, and splurge on a designer handbag when your budget allows. You will have these pieces for a long time.
- Don't pile on prints. Wear a print with a solid color for balance.
- Be comfortable in your clothes. Avoid fabrics that are overly tight, clingy, or crease easily.
- Skinny jeans do not look good on everyone. Stretchy, slightly low-rise jeans in a dark hue are elongating and slimming. Avoid skirts and dresses that are poufy and bubble shaped unless you want to look like a balloon.
- Allow yourself plenty of time when shopping for jeans, swimwear, and undergarments. It takes time to find the perfect size and fit.
- Shorts look best on the young, slender, and cellulite free. Belted high waist denim shorts worn with a fanny pack and visor should be banished from the planet. Wear calf length cargo pants instead.

Resources: Love Your Body

Books

Women's Bodies, Women's Wisdom, by Christiane Northrup, M.D. (Bantam, 1998)

The Wisdom of Menopause, by Christiane Northrup, M.D. (Bantam, 2001)

Eating Right for a Bad Gut, by Dr. James Scala (Plume, 1990)

The Sexy Years, by Suzanne Somers (Three Rivers Press, 2004)

Tired of Being Tired, by Jesse Lynn Hanley, M.D., and Nancy Deville (Berkley, 2001)

Beauty Evolution, by Bobbi Brown (Harper Collins, 2002)

Alkalize or Die, by Dr. Theodore A. Baroody (Holographic Health Press, 1991)

The Cure, by Dr. Timothy Brantley (Wiley, 2007)

The Ultimate Soup Bible, Consultant Editor: Anne Sheasby (Barnes & Noble, 2005)

Passion for Pasta, by Antonio Carluccio (Cole, 1994)

Making Faces, by Kevin Aucoin (Little, Brown, 1997)

Face Forward, by Kevin Aucoin (Little, Brown, 2000)

Product List

Target's White Strips

L'Oreal Preference Hair Color

Zerran Negate Hair Care

Splish Splash Shampoo by Circle of Friends

Neutrogena Clean Replenishing Shampoo

Aveda Shampure

Conair Instant Heating Hairsetter

Bumble & Bumble Hair Powder

Hair Mascara by Rashelle

Men Only Mustache Dye

Vitamin A derivatives—Retin A—Tazorac and Renova

Neutrogena Healthy Skin Anti-Wrinkle Serum

Burt Bees Repair Serum

DHC Organic Facial Olive Oil

DHC Deep Cleansing Oil

Cetaphil Facial Cleanser

Barielle Nail Strengthener

Miracle Foot Repair

Burt Bees Coconut Foot Cream

Finishing Touch Micro Razor for Women

Laura Mercier Secret Camouflage Concealer

Sonia Kashuk for Target—Concealer Palette

Bobbi Brown Creamy Concealer and Stick Foundation

Mac Stick Foundation and Face Powder

Clarins Super Restorative Tinted Cream SPF 20

Bare Escentuals—bare Minerals Foundation

Clinique Super Moisture Makeup

Jergens Natural Glow Daily Moisturizer

Sephora makeup brushes

Sonia Kashuk for Target—makeup brushes

Shu Uemera Eyelash Curler

Eden Blend Rice & Soy Beverage

Teeccino caffeine-free herbal coffee

Green Vibrance—organic green superfood

Yogi Tea Company—Stomach Ease Tea

Traditional Medicinals—Smooth Move Tea

Bio K Acidophilus

Spanx and Donna Karan Figure Slimming Undergarments

Barely There and Wacoal Brassieres

Nourish Your Spirit

MEDITATION

The only journey is the one within.

—Rilke

I have always been a traveler, but no journey has ultimately been more rewarding and at times challenging than the journey within. I have been meditating for twenty-seven years, and

A moment of peace in this crazy world is such a blessing.

personally I don't know how to stay sane without it. Research shows that meditation is one of the most direct and effective ways to reverse aging and improve your overall health. It is that powerful. It is also the most potent beauty secret you will ever find and available to anyone willing to learn a few simple guidelines.

Meditation is the process by which we learn to go beyond the constant chatter of the mind to the deep place of calm that resides within each of us. It guides us to the place within ourselves that is untouched by the traumas we all encounter at times. We become a witness to our lives, instead of being overwhelmed by the ongoing drama.

As you learn to meditate, you will acquire the wisdom and equanimity to deal with the big storms that come up, and you will feel less troubled by the petty ups and downs that are out of your control. You will feel more distance between events and your reactions to them. Someone cuts you off in traffic—no big deal. An eagerly anticipated romantic date falls through at the last minute—well, it happens sometimes.

A priceless daily habit

Everything in your life will be greatly enhanced when you make regular meditation a daily habit. Your life will begin to look and feel better, and so will you. It will help you feel both relaxed and energized. A calm focused mind will also help improve your memory and concentration, and help you sleep better too. If you want a healthier mind (and who doesn't), learn to meditate.

According to a report in the May edition of *More* magazine, studies at the Mind/Body Institute have shown that "women who did 15–20 minutes a day of some kind of meditative activity reported a 58% reduction in premenstrual symptoms, significant decreases in hot flash intensity, and 90% were able to reduce or eliminate use of sleep medications." The study also revealed that in addition to reducing physical symptoms, meditators had a more positive attitude about their bodies' changes with fewer anxieties and negative thoughts.

Just as there is more than one way to quiet the mind and relax the body, if you are not familiar with meditation, you might feel more comfortable calling it *going within, calming your mind,* or *centering yourself.* All healing begins from this center of peace within you, whether the goal is to counteract stress, develop healthy relationships, or find more purpose and passion in your life. And these are just some of the physical and emotional benefits. The spiritual rewards go even deeper.

> *From my experiences on studies on people using meditation, it has been established that long- term meditators can have a biological age between five and twelve years younger than their chronological age.*
>
> —Deepak Chopra

Going mainstream

Meditation is now becoming so popular and mainstream that even major athletes and artists of all genres include a time of *centering* as part of their training. It is practiced in hospitals, prisons, and Fortune 500 companies. The National Center for Complementary and Alternative Medicine estimates that more than fifteen million Americans practice regular meditation. No wonder, with all these health benefits.

It is no longer viewed as a weird practice that only vegan, tree-hugging, Los Angeles or Berkeley dwelling, new age junkies, or old hippies are into. It is not about intense mystical flight or out of body experience, though that may happen to some people. Meditation, in its most basic form, is the moment-by-moment awareness of the breath and practical way to quiet the restless mind. One thing that makes meditation so appealing to lots of people is that it is religiously neutral, which makes it particularly attractive to the religiously impaired like myself. Even atheists and agnostics can sign up if they'd like.

It's also one of those things you can learn at any age and practice anytime and anywhere with guaranteed results. When friends ask me what I do to stay looking young, the first thing I always tell them is to learn to meditate before anything else, and then do all the other things. If you want the clear-eyed glow and sparkle more often associated with one in the early flush of youth, then meditation is the way. It will do more for you than any beauty product or cosmetic

Make time for the one essential that is too important to do without.

procedure you can buy, any book you might read, or any workshop you may attend. Even ten minutes twice a day can have a significant impact that will be well worth your time and effort.

The world, with all its demands, will try and convince you that you don't have enough time for meditation. With so many health benefits, you don't have time *not* to meditate. It's that vital to your overall health. We give too much time to nonessentials in life—the average American spends nine years of his or her life watching television. What a waste of our valuable time.

A day that begins and ends with the peace of meditation is a life-altering, mind-changing, joy-inviting way to extend your life. It takes time and energy to create bad habits, so why not spend the time creating a positive habit that has potential to change and enrich your life in remarkable ways? Meditation may help us stay youthful, but it can also help us to recognize and value our wisdom and maturity that are by-products of aging.

A sacred place inside of you

If you want the truth, I'll tell you the truth:
listen to the secret sound, the real sound,
which is inside you.

—Kabir

There is a place inside you that is supremely wise, a place where truth and intuition and infinite knowing abide. Call it the voice of Spirit, call it the voice of your inner guide, or call it the voice of God. What name you give it is not important. Sometimes the voice will be loud and clear. Other times it may be a soft whisper. Through meditation, you will learn to recognize this infinitely loving voice.

You will be given the gift of clarity and clear thinking, and your life will be transformed. We can only hear this inner voice when the mud of our thoughts settles, and we are quiet enough to be receptive. Then you will begin to feel a peace so sweet and blissful, you may indeed wonder how you ever lived without it.

No matter how busy my life may be some days, I always make time for meditation as it helps everything in my day run smoother. One of the great things about meditation is that you can practice it anywhere at anytime. One of my favorite times to meditate is during one of those tiresome long flights when people usually assume I'm sleeping.

If I have a long hectic day and can't make it home to meditate, then I sometimes sit in my car for a few minutes to breathe deep and center myself. I have pulled over to the side of the road at times when I am starting to feel stressed in the middle of a busy day, and I have even escaped to public toilets to sneak a few moments of sanity—restoring, silent contemplation.

Keep a secret chamber of silence within yourself, where you will not let moods, trials, battles, or inharmony enter. Keep out all hatred, vengefulness, and desires.
In this chamber of peace, God will visit you.

—Paramahansa Yogananda

The unruly mind

When you first start to meditate, the mind will seem even more unruly than usual. Don't worry. Expect it even. Our minds are so full of relentless chatter that it often seems that the mind has a mind of its own. When your mind starts to wander in meditation, just gently keep bringing it back to center. Observe the thoughts, but without judgment bring your attention back to the breath and relax.

When I have a particularly restless meditation, I try not to judge it as good or bad, for I know that I always benefit on some level. You may also experience boredom and physical discomfort. This will usually fade as you become more familiar with the process of meditation. Meditation may be simple but not always easy, so I've listed some basic guidelines to help you get started.

- The key is to set aside a certain time every morning and night, and do your best to stick to that schedule. Try to meditate in the same place each time, as you will gradually create a calm spiritual vibration that will make it easier to go within.
- A good way to prepare the body for meditation is to tense and relax the muscles in each body part. You can do this sitting in a sturdy chair or standing. Simply tense the muscle, hold tightly for a few seconds, and release. Feel the energy vibrating there, energizing and revitalizing your entire body. The principle of tensing and relaxing the body has been popularly endorsed and used by medical science as an aid in many maladies, including the reduction of nervous anxiety and high blood pressure. You can try this several times, and after each release let out a deep breath.
- You might want to prepare an altar and light candles or incense. Put anything you want on the altar that holds spiritual meaning to you. I keep a photo of my mum and my dog Whiskey, my spiritual teachers, a small Buddha, and a few inspirational books that I read from before I begin my meditation. Meditate in comfortable clothes, and you might like to place a lightweight cotton or wool shawl around your shoulders or over your chair.
- Before I begin my meditation, I like to take a warm bath as part of my morning practice. It helps me have less aches and pains and maintain a comfortable position, thus helping my meditation.
- In general, most people sit for meditation. If you sit in a chair, sit with both feet flat on

the floor and hands resting gently in your lap. You may also sit upright and cross-legged on a firm mat if that is comfortable for you. Sometimes I sit cross-legged on the floor, but if I intend to have a long meditation, I find it much more comfortable to sit in a chair.

- Keep the spine straight and elongated, shoulders relaxed, and chin parallel to the floor. Let go of any tension in the face or jaw. Hands can be placed gently in your lap, right hand on top of the left with thumbs touching.

- Close your eyes and perhaps start with a short prayer. Use any words that are meaningful to you.

- Breathe in for seven to ten seconds, hold for seven to ten seconds, and then release the breath on the same amount. This breathing exercise helps to slow the breath and focus your mind in preparation for meditation.

- Now breathe regularly through the nose. Observe the breath going in and out. Pay attention to the space between each breath. If you get distracted and start thinking of all the bills you have to pay or the vanilla soy latte you are craving, don't get discouraged and just do the best you can.

- The more you practice meditation, the more your body and mind will remember the process and the easier it will be to slip back into it. You may want to start with a few minutes at first and then build up as you go along. As you create the habit of regular meditation, you will gradually be able to increase the duration of your session.

- I like to meditate first thing in the morning when it is quiet and before the world and life demands my attention. I meditate about thirty to forty-five minutes, and then again for about twenty minutes before dinner. Some people like to meditate before they go to bed, but I usually end up sleeping instead, which is not meditation.

- Do what works for you, but remember that it is usually best to start the day with a meditation, no matter how short, as it sets the tone of your day. I also take any opportunity I can throughout the day to refresh myself with a few moments of silence and deep breathing.

Strive to close the eyes of the body and open those of the soul
and look into your own heart.

—St. Teresa of Avila

FAITH

Faith is the substance of things hoped for,
the evidence of things not seen.

—New Testament, Hebrews 11:1

What does it mean to have faith, and who and what do we have faith in? I once heard faith described in this way, as being *faith in good without a speck of evidence*. As we age, many of us, with more years behind us than ahead, start to have moments of existential angst that often jolt us awake in the wee early hours of the morning. If you haven't already spent some significant time in introspection, these moments can send you into a midlife panic. We begin to question our faith or, rather, the lack of it. We want an answer to the big

Sometimes we just want to know that we and our loved ones are going to be okay.

question about the purpose of our lives, and we want assurance of what lies ahead.

If we knew in advance exactly what lies around the corner, then we'd have no need for faith. Unfortunately, however, that is not how life works at any age. Faith, then, is the belief in that which you cannot yet see or know. What I do know for sure is that your faith will be as personal and intimate to you as mine is to me.

For me, faith works best on a day-by-day basis. I think about the future, but I focus on the present and let God take care of the rest. I have deep faith that God in Her infinite wisdom always, without exception, has my best interests in mind, though my ego may beg to differ at times. I also believe that our lives are governed by a divine order that is playing out exactly the way it is supposed to, whether we believe it to be so or not.

A leap of faith

We've all had significant times in our lives when we've been called on to take what is commonly referred to as a *leap of faith*—times when we have no rational evidence besides our own highest hopes and our divinely attuned intuition. When I moved to Los Angeles from Tokyo to be with Alan, I really had no idea if it would work out, though I knew I had to find out. The same thing was true when I moved from England to Tokyo. On both occasions I expected things to work out well in some way or another, but I was not overly attached to how that would look. I trusted that the inner nudging that guided me to risk and move forward was the voice of God within me.

When I felt afraid of putting one foot in front of the next, this presence within me became my polestar and compass in everything I did and continue to do. Think of a time in your life when you took a leap of faith and trusted the inner nudging that propelled you to make a positive life change.

> *Back of every creation, supporting it like an arch, is faith.*
> *Enthusiasm is nothing: it comes and goes.*
> *But if one believes, then miracles occur.*

> —Henry Miller

I believe that our deepest soul yearnings are but a preview of what the future holds for us. I'm not talking about material desires, but something much deeper that stirs us to create and risk when we have no real evidence apart from an inner voice that beckons us to dream and trust. Having a vision in mind of what we want to draw into our reality invites that experience into manifestation sooner than it might otherwise. But we still have to do the other part, like taking the action steps.

I may hold a vision of seeing the finished product of a book I wrote smiling back at me from the shelves of my local bookstore, but if I don't sit down and write everyday, it is not going to happen. If you want to start a new business but don't do the research and the groundwork, it probably won't happen. I've also experienced the opposite, where I have had no fixed or specific vision, and things just showed up in my life better than I could have ever imagined. So go figure. Life can be a contradiction. I think the key is to be open, flexible, and trust and then see what unfolds.

Pay attention to the signs

We do get signs along the way that permit us a glimpse of our destinies, even when it seems far fetched and highly unlikely. Despite my meager beginnings, I always knew I would travel the world. I don't know how I knew—I just knew. How all that was going to happen, I had no idea.

At fifteen I won a contest called Miss Fuji Film that was sponsored by a small local camera store. I remember that day very clearly. After I won, my dad and I were walking through the town talking about the events of the day, and on the way to catch the number 83 bus home, he turned to me and said, "Well, Angela, the next thing you know, you'll be off to Japan." I looked at him as if he had just said the most insanely ridiculous thing ever, something only a parent would say, and so I mumbled something along the lines of "Oh yeah right, Dad, me going to Japan."

And that is exactly what happened. A year later, I won Miss Teen England and was on my way to Tokyo to represent England in Miss Teen International. That experience led me to live in Japan for eight years where I met Alan when he and his group were on their first Asian tour all those years ago. I could not have imagined all of that in my wildest dreams.

Granted, not all signs are so clear and overt; some are much more subtle and quiet, but they do happen all the time. We just need to pay attention and get out of the way of how we think life is supposed to be. I love surprises (the good ones, of course) because we never know what magic might await us. Do you remember a sign that significantly set the direction of your life? Was there a time in your life when a vision became a reality, and what did it look and feel like?

Spiritual community

For the past twenty-seven years, Alan and I have been blessed to be part of the spiritual community of Self Realization Fellowship at Lake Shrine in Los Angeles. We were married there on the Gandhi Memorial Lawn all those years ago, and since that time, it has been a treasured part of our lives. Alan was raised Jewish, and I Catholic, but we were both drawn to Eastern religion long before we even met. It spoke to us in ways that our childhood religions did not. My years in Japan exposed me to Zen Buddhism and Transcendental Meditation, and Alan studied everything from Jewish Mysticism to the Upanishads.

The wonderful thing about Lake Shrine, besides its sheer, breathtaking physical beauty, is that it is a center that honors all religions. This has always been very important to us. We serve there, meditate there, and have met some of our dearest friends there. We honor Alan's Judaic heritage by celebrating the Jewish holidays, and we celebrate Easter and Christmas as well as special and auspicious times of other religions in between.

Prayer and butter lips

You may well be wondering how prayer and butter lips go together. Trust me, they do, as you will soon find out. As a child, the formal prayers I repeated by rote at Sunday mass felt forced and rigid. Confessing my sins every Saturday to an imperfect priest sitting in a confessional box dispensing six Hail Marys felt dodgy, even back then. I've never had time for a religion that used fear to control. And yet, I always had a deep longing to be closer to the loving God that somehow I sensed was at the core of everything and everyone.

The function of prayer is not to influence God, but rather to
change the nature of one who prays.

—Soren Kierkegard

I also loved the intense musky scent of incense, devotional hymns, and yes, on occasion the hot parish priests. This is where the juicy part comes in. When I was in my early teens and obsessed with the butter-lipped flirty Father Bishop, I even fantasized about becoming a nun. In my warped juvenile mind, I reasoned that if I became a nun, then Father Bishop and I could declare our undying love for each other, and then run off together some place and live happily ever after—like Saint Francis and Saint Claire, but with the sex and without eternal damnation.

More importantly, I would get to live out my cherished fantasy of gliding over the Yorkshire moors—okay, they're not exactly the Austrian alps, but they'd have to suffice—singing "The Hills Are Alive" like Maria from *The Sound of Music*, while luscious lips looked on adoringly in the distance.

In my real life, once I began to talk to the Divine in the language of my own heart, prayer became my daily conversation with God. For me, deep focused prayer is a form of meditation. I talk to God all the time—when I'm at the gym, cleaning dishes, or in my car waiting for the lights to change. God is my constant companion who never judges when I fall short and loves me unconditionally no matter what.

Sometimes my prayers are long and reverential; at other times the best and most sincere prayer I can come up with is a brief but heart-felt *thank you, my God, thank you, thank you, I love you.* And on occasion I have the existential *I don't know why this is the way it is, but I know you do and that has to be enough* prayer.

Fate and free will

I have been thinking about this a lot lately—the dance between destiny and free will. It seems to me that certain things are predestined, but we also have choice. Another one of life's contradictions, but perhaps both are happening simultaneously and in harmony with each other.

The challenge in life is to not worry about the things we can't control and to take responsibility for the things we can. Things like where we are born, who our parents are, and whether one ends up living in Japan for many years definitely seem to be karmic things to me. But it is the daily moment-to-moment choices we make that affect how we steer and move through life. This is where free will and faith come in.

We can choose how we respond to life—the good, the bad, and the in-between. We can choose to see the misfortunes in life as an excuse to live in fear, or we can choose faith. Faith is always a choice, though not always the easy or comfortable one. To me, faith is trust in a friendly universe that is essentially good despite the inevitable challenges in life that we all encounter. Faith is also the security that I have the strength and resilience to face anything that life may bring me.

Questioning is good

It's not the answer that enlightens,
but the question.

—Decouvertes

I believe all of the above most of the time, but sometimes I still have my own moments of existential angst where I question everything, including God. Maybe it's turning fifty and my inner skeptic is not so easily appeased. I look at the world and all the suffering and unrest, and I honestly wonder if God didn't make some serious mistakes when He or She created this crazy world of duality. Sometimes I pray and wonder if anyone is listening, or if it is indeed a deluded, one-sided conversation in my own head.

When I see the sorrows of the world, I wonder if everything happens randomly and with the luck of how the cards fall. Of course I know it's not. I have experienced way too many moments of divine synchronistic grace and plentiful blessings to believe otherwise.

And yet I still question, for I believe that questioning is necessary for the building of faith, even though it is uncomfortable being a doubting Thomas. Within me is a deep knowingness that trusts even when my mind seemingly doesn't. Perhaps I will always question. Maybe it's just my nature, but it has occurred to me that age has brought with it the blessing that I no longer question myself. I am like the turtle at ease in my own shell. I have faith in myself. And even when I feel melancholy and lost, my sadness sometimes feels like a familiar friend, as valuable and as much a part of me as my joy.

Explaining the unexplainable

Faith is nothing but a living, wide-awake consciousness of God within.

—Gandhi

Atheists proclaim that people of faith use God as a buffer against the sorrows and challenges of life, instead of relying on themselves. I say that life can be tough, and if I and others find comfort in our relationship with the Divine, well I see that as a blessing and not a weakness. I've always thought of my relationship with Spirit as a partnership. So in a sense, when I find comfort and strength from God, who lives within me, I am in fact drawing upon a strength and resilience from within myself—my highest self, that is.

Over the years, I have stopped looking to the world as an external means to give me peace and joy. I enjoy life and its many exquisite, earthly pleasures, but a moment of peace is worth more to me than anything material. What a relief when I understood that the peace and joy I have always been searching for is inside me—always has been, always will be. Joy is an inside job.

No one can give it to you or take it from you. It is yours for the keeping. You don't need to learn anything new, apart from meditation, to access this joy and peace. In fact, most of us need to unlearn much of what we have been told to be the truth when we were children by generally well-meaning but misinformed adults at church, school, and home.

Faith helps us feel whole and sustains us beyond our pain and limited human understanding.

Faith helps us to move forward with courage, especially when we face the pain of difficult times. Faith, however, is somewhat different from hope. Hope is focused on a specific desired outcome. When those hopes and expectations are not met, disappointment and dissolution often set in. Faith is different. It is trust in the great flow of life and the replenishing grace of God.

I also believe in karma and reincarnation. In saying this, however, I in no way use it as a trite means to explain what often seems as random, horrific suffering in our world. That said, these Eastern principles make sense to my way of thinking, and often, though not always, explain the unexplainable. I believe there is a karmic system that, based on the law of cause and effect, works things out in a manner that is hard for our human minds and hearts to grasp.

It seems to me that our lessons in life are customized in ways that may not make sense to us, and yet I believe in the great big cosmic scheme of things, they do. I trust in this, and it brings me peace. Age has given me the ability relax with all the stuff in life that I don't understand. I choose not to lose sleep over what may or may not happen in my life. I believe that however life unfolds, it will continue to be for my highest good, one way or another.

Possessing faith is not convenient. You still have to live it.

—Francoise Mallet-Jori

SILENCE AND SOLITUDE

One of the greatest sounds of them all—and to me it is a sound—is utter complete silence.

—Andre Kostelanetz

We are not raised to view silence and solitude as gifts, but rather as a form of punishment. As a child, I remember being sent to my room to be alone when I misbehaved. How funny that as I've aged, going to my room to be quiet and alone is one of my most favorite things to do. My office is where I work, but my bedroom is where I unwind and recharge.

I meditate and I make love there, but mostly I just enjoy the quietness of reading or writing in my journal. In the evening after a busy day, I enjoy the ritual of taking a bath and then lighting candles in my bedroom in preparation for meditation or a pre-dinner nap.

I know many women who live busy, hectic lives filled with activity and caring for others, but often with very little time left for themselves. This is why it's so important that you find some time in each day to be alone and silent. Take whatever time you can, even if it's fifteen minutes or an hour. Make that your special time, but instead of turning on the television or the computer, why not spend that time alone, quiet, and without distractions. Ask yourself if it is really necessary to check your e-mail several times a day, and when you're in the car, practice driving without the radio on for a change.

Turn on the answering machine and put a do not disturb sign on your door, if you need to.

I used to be one of those people who kept the television on all the time for company. The comfort of another's voice in the background made me feel less alone and afraid. I don't know what I was afraid of back then in my late teens and twenties. Turning off the television meant that I'd have to start learning to listen to what needed to be heard within myself. Like most people, I had contained and hid a lifetime of little fears that demanded attention when I was silent and alone.

I measure my emotional healing and personal growth in part to how comfortable I am with myself when I am alone. It is a liberating realization to acknowledge how far I have come and how much I have grown. I just needed to grow up and make peace with parts of myself that were demanding some care and healing. Then silence and solitude became a pleasurable treat, and not something to be afraid of.

Besides meditation and the quiet peaceful sanctuary of my bedroom, I also enjoy long, solitary walks on the beach. In the summer, I love to sit out by my pool and watch the visiting hummingbirds, squirrels, and butterflies busily doing their thing. Do what works best for you. Most people enjoy communing with nature in some way. For me it's about taking time to escape the hustle and buzz of modern living so I can slow down enough to really relax and unwind.

> *If we have not quietness in our minds, outward comfort will do*
> *no more for us than a golden slipper on a gouty foot.*
>
> —John Bunyon

Highly stressed and overstimulated

Speeding through life is very stressful. Twenty-four hours a day we are bombarded by constant noise and the overstimulation of our senses. In our modern world, it is very hard to shut out the external din that's going on all around us. Everywhere we go, there's continuous noise and lights that are way too bright. No wonder many of us feel overwhelmed by modern living. I will walk out of a restaurant or store if the noise is too loud. Many people seem to have built up a tolerance or immunity to it, but not I.

The older I get, the more quietness I need. I am an HSP—a highly sensitive person, that is, in reference to Dr. Elaine N. Aron's bestselling book, *The Highly Sensitive Person*. I'm not sensitive in the way that I am shy or highly emotional, but I am definitely sensitive when it comes to having a sensitive nervous system. According to Dr. Aron, an HSP can be easily overwhelmed to the point of exhaustion when one is bombarded by intense sights and sounds. I have more girlfriends than not who also consider themselves to be HSPs, so I know I'm not alone. I used to think of my overwired nervous system as a defect, but since I read Dr. Aron's book, I have learned to protect and value this trait as a cherished part of myself.

Think of time alone as an investment in your health and your sanity.

Decades ago, people did not get diseases like Mononucleosis and the chronic fatigue symptoms in Epstein Barr disease. Modern technology has brought amazing new innovations, but with it a society that is highly stressed and overstimulated. I live a relatively low-tech life. I use a cell phone sparingly and have no desire to learn how to text message, even though my phone apparently comes with lots of *extras*. I do not need these *extras* and do not share my husband's excitement about all the latest new toys and gadgets.

I have learned to use the computer for basic stuff like checking my e-mails and writing my books. I enjoy television and other electronics that don't require much mental energy to figure out how to use. I prefer an on/off switch, and that's about it. Any more than that confuses my sensitive brain. TiVo is the one exception, as it allows me to watch some quality television without all those intrusive commercials. The key with anything in life is to find what works for you and discard the rest.

You must learn to be still in the midst of activity and to be vibrantly alive in repose.

—Indira Gandhi

Recharge on the go

When I'm traveling and on the go, I always try to find a place, whether it's a park or quiet cafe, where I can restore and maintain my sense of peace and calm. This is especially true when I travel to places with a higher energy than my usual surroundings, like New York and Tokyo, for example. I love New York for about a week. Any longer and I think I would go insane from the unrelenting noise.

Of course Tokyo can be incredibly manic too, and yet the Japanese still manage to keep a sense of tranquility amidst the chaos. It stems from learning to live in very small spaces while honoring each other's space. I will admit it is hard to feel peaceful when you are shoved into a subway train like sardines at the height of Tokyo rush hour—something I try and avoid at all cost.

Still, Tokyo has something of everything that I love. It is filled with culture, fashion, and great restaurants (you can taste some of the best pasta outside of Italy in Tokyo). On the same street as all of the above, you might also find a beautiful ancient temple, a tiny tea garden hidden away, or, if you are lucky to be there in spring, a park filled with beautiful pink cherry blossom trees. Day spas are everywhere—at the train station and along every high street—waiting for you to come in for a quick foot rub or shoulder massage followed by a cup of herbal tea. One can enjoy a half hour of rest and quiet contemplation in the midst of a frenzied afternoon of shopping.

This works for me. The social and cultural pace of Italy also works for me. In Florence, when I reached my level of sensory overload from too much shopping and too many people, I would escape into one of many churches that could be found in most piazzas. After twenty minutes of silence, I would emerge refreshed and ready for a gelato and more shopping.

Practice the art of being

What am I doing? Nothing. I am letting life rain upon me.

—Rahel Varnhagen

Over the years, I have treated myself to an annual, five-day silent retreat. Usually it takes me a few days to settle in with the silence. Sometimes it seems that once my thoughts have settled, it's time to leave the retreat. My mouth may have stopped chattering, but my mind compensates and works overtime. There are no phones or televisions, no e-mails to check, and no fashion magazines to idle away the time. I am alone with no distractions but my thoughts. I meditate and pray and sometimes I read and write. Mostly I try to practice the art of *being*. I attempt to leave my cares and concerns behind, as I know they will be there for me to reclaim again when I leave the retreat—if I so choose, that is.

People often comment to me that they can't imagine being silent with nothing *to do* for five days. The thought of withdrawing from the world in such a way invokes anxiety, not calm. It does not sound fun to some people, but a silent retreat nourishes and restores me in a way that other pleasures do not. No matter what is going on in my life, I always leave a retreat renewed and energized. I'm also a lot nicer to be around, so my loved ones reap the rewards too.

You can make silence part of your life and spiritual practice without going away on retreat. Whenever you can, take a day or an afternoon away from the demands of the world to be silent and alone. Take time out for you. Silence enables us to slip into more focused activities with optimum results. A mind that is allowed to rest is ultimately more productive than a mind that is frazzled and nerves that are frayed.

We are born alone and shall die alone, so we may as well get used to our own company.

Our full power and potential is awakened through silence and drained away in endless chatter. I love good stimulating conversation, but it's amazing the time and energy we waste in mindless talking. Quietness in the mind is nourished from an outer environment of peacefulness that we create for ourselves. Getting comfortable with silence and solitude is where you start.

Solitude

I was never less alone than when by myself.

—Edward Gibbon

The thought of actually choosing to be alone and thriving because of it is quite unsettling for many women of any age. Being alone is not an unfortunate thing, but rather a lovely declaration of self-care and appreciation. I enjoy going out to the movies and dinner alone, though I do choose restaurants where I feel comfortable and welcomed as a party of one. I'm not likely to go to a restaurant alone at 8:00 p.m. on a Saturday night when I know it will be filled with couples or groups of friends. When I stayed in Florence alone last fall, I would usually eat in a fine restaurant for lunch and grab something light at a cafe in the evening on my way back to my hotel. Or if there was a particular restaurant I really wanted to try one evening, I'd go early before the crowds came.

Yes, there were some occasions when I'd pass a restaurant that was filled with people happily eating and drinking and I'd feel a twinge of loneliness. For a fleeting moment, I'd wish Alan, Arielle, or a friend were with me to share a fabulous meal together. Fortunately, there are numerous occasions in my life where I share many memorable meals with loved ones, and I always make a note of places I come across when I am alone to share with them at a later time.

> *What a desire! ... To live in peace with that word: Myself.*
>
> —Sylvia Ashton-Warner

I am not sad, lonely, or antisocial; I just enjoy doing certain things alone some of the time. I appreciate togetherness and aloneness, and think that each one enhances the other. People sometimes confuse aloneness with loneliness, but they are very different. I have felt very alone in large groups of people and at times in intimate relationships. More often than not, I feel quite content and self-sufficient when I am alone. I have become a very kind and loving companion to myself.

I'm not what you would call a *people person,* but I think people are wonderful and interesting in small doses. I don't usually tire of my own company, but if I do, or I am feeling troubled about something and need to talk it out, I never hesitate to reach out for the company of others. What a marvelous thing self-acceptance is!

In many cultures silence and solitude are built into daily life.

Alan travels for business about five months spread out over the course of a year. It is what he does. Sometimes I travel with him if it is feasible and intriguing to me, but we do have to spend a lot of time apart. I have learned the value of being alone out of necessity. At first, it was very difficult to be apart, though quite understandable, in a new marriage. I do believe, though unconsciously at the time, that I chose this kind of relationship in order for me to grow and strengthen in ways that may have been difficult with a traditional nine-to-five husband. Quite honestly, I don't know how well I would do with a full-time husband, even one as fine and exceptional as the one I am fortunate to have.

> *Sometimes I wonder if men and women really suit each other.*
> *Perhaps they should live next door and just visit now and then.*
>
> —Katherine Hepburn

Learning to be self-sufficient

A friend of mine has a guesthouse where she works and escapes to whenever she needs as does her husband of many years. She swears by it and says it's one of the main reasons why her long marriage works as well as it does. Not every woman can have her own separate guesthouse, of course, but I think we all need a room or space of our own.

Self-sufficiency in a woman is a very attractive quality, and most importantly, it fosters a sense of empowerment when one knows how to enjoy and value her own company first. We then enjoy others more. When we come together with friends and loved ones, it is because we choose to, and not because we are needy and desperate. Instead of wondering about the emotional wellness of people who enjoy their own company, perhaps we should be concerned about the person who can never be alone.

It may be hard to find quiet time for yourself when you have children at home and many demands on your time. But with a bit of planning and making yourself a priority, it can be done. There are times in life when we need more solitude, and other times when we need more connection with the dear ones in our lives.

After my mum died and Alan and I returned to Los Angeles from England, what I craved most were endless days of quiet time alone. I had nothing inside of me to give to others. I needed to replenish myself and go deep into my sadness and grief without thought of needing to be there for anyone else. As it turned out, Alan had to leave for business for three weeks, and Arielle had just left to start her first year at college. So I spent three invaluable weeks home alone with my two loyal dogs as my comfort and companions.

You don't need others to fill you up. You can do that for yourself.

With the little energy I had, I walked the dogs twice a day, made myself simple light meals, wept and prayed frequently, and wrote in my journal in between. Alan and Arielle called often, as did my concerned friends, but for the most part I remained quiet and alone—just as I wanted and needed.

I have never found the companion that was so companionable as solitude.

—Henry David Thoreau

Going on retreat

A month or so later, I got it in my head that it would be good for my healing to go away to my usual, silent retreat. I drove down to Encinitas in the pouring rain, and I cried all the way. I had arranged to be at the retreat for five days. It soon became clear to me, however, after the first sleepless, anguished night alone, that I was in the midst of high anxiety, not peace and calm.

Instead of being okay with that, I tried to convince myself that I should stay and needed to be strong. I had never left a retreat early before and saw it as a weakness if I did. How unrelentingly harsh we can be toward ourselves sometimes. What I really wanted was to be home with my family. I needed the comfort and reassurance of their love and support around me. Fortunately, a wise nun at the retreat noticed how troubled I was. In the group meditation and at dinner, I could not contain my tears. I was coming undone in front of everyone.

Obviously, I was not okay. The nun called me aside and asked me if I needed counseling. Of course, then I really lost it and sobbed my way through telling her about my mum dying, and how conflicted I felt about whether I should leave the retreat or not. She was an older woman with very tender, motherly eyes. I felt such a relief just telling her my story, and even more relieved when she told me the wisest thing to do was to go home and be with my loved ones.

Sometimes, she told me, silent retreats are exactly what we need, but other times, the best medicine, especially when we are grieving, is to be with our families. I quickly packed my bag and called Alan. I never call home when I am on retreat, so he was very concerned when he heard *We need both aloneness and togetherness to be whole.* me crying on the phone. He actually drove all the way down to Encinitas so we could drive caravan-style home to L.A. I thought a retreat would be good for me, but I had never lost a beloved parent before.

To be alone is to be adult.

—Jean Rostand

No empty nest

When Arielle graduated from college last summer, I was thrilled to have her live back home after being away for four years. It was also an adjustment for me. I did not experience the *empty nest syndrome* when she left for college. Not that I didn't miss her. Of course I did. But we spoke daily and visited her in Berkeley, or she would come home for a weekend at least once a month. Her return home, however, was in some ways a challenge for me at times. I found the constant energy around the house took some getting used to after four years of my own space. It had nothing to do with how much I love her and welcomed her presence, but simply a matter of what I had grown accustomed to.

I also found that I worried about her more after moving home than when she was living far away in Siena or Berkeley. I know many mothers who can relate to this. There is less angst when you can't see what you're kid is up to than when you're living under the same roof. I worried about her driving, though I did not, like some mothers, stay up late waiting for her to come home. I paid my staying up late dues when she was an infant.

I am happy to say that we worked out any kinks in our living arrangement, so that the three of us have our space when we need it. She has a full and busy life, so I still get to have my alone time with the added pleasure of looking forward to her coming home each day. It's been a joy having her around, and I hope she will stay until she can afford to move into her own place.

> *Silence and solitude are vital to knowing yourself, and necessary for creative expression and unleashing your imagination.*

I still worry when she is out driving, but I just say a shield of protection prayer for her when she leaves the house.

There is a tendency for some creative people to isolate and stay cloistered at home for days on end. I need uninterrupted time alone, but after weeks spent sitting in front of the computer, I am ready to be out in the world observing life and connecting with others. I could spend hours people watching, and then wondering what their stories are. My journal becomes my companion when I travel, and I enjoy being a witness to the spectacle of life going on around me. Life experiences and the many thoughts that pass through my mind become fuel for my writing practice.

> *I was alone with all that could happen.*
>
> —William Gass

Aloneness and togetherness

In America, we tend to view people who enjoy aloneness to be shy, emotionally stunted, or introverted. Not the case—with me anyway. I can be the life of the party when I choose to be, but I don't need long lists of friends to sustain me. I value aloneness, but I like knowing that there are people near by if I need them (and cafes and restaurants if I need them too).

Basically I'm a city girl, but one who doesn't want the noise of someone living on the floor above me. Been there, done that, and believe me, it's no fun having your upstairs neighbor screaming at her husband on a Sunday mornings or belting out opera at 3:00 a.m. One of our old neighbors upstairs was comedian Shecky Green, and boy did he love to sing opera in the bath or shower—usually in those wee early hours when I was trying to get my beauty sleep.

We need a balance of solitude and togetherness to be whole, and only you can know what works best for your innate temperament. You have to find what feeds and replenishes you at any given time. Then, let the peace and beauty of silence soothe and comfort you. And may solitude remind you of the power and strength that lie at the core of your being, waiting to be revealed and revered.

Do not be afraid to embrace the arms of loneliness.
Do not be concerned with the thorns of solitude.
Why worry that you will miss something?
Learn to be at home with yourself without a hand to hold
Learn to endure isolation with only the stars for friends
… Beauty arises from the ashes of despair
Solitude brings the clarity of still waters
Wisdom completes the circle of your dreams.

—Nancy Wood

GRATITUDE AND SERVICE

*In daily life, we must remind ourselves that it is not happiness that
makes us grateful but gratefulness that makes us happy.*

—Brother Steindl-Rast

I have many blessings in my life, but the one that greatly affects the quality of my life, especially
as I have gotten older, is my ability to be grateful. When I was a child my family was poor,
and I didn't feel grateful for much of anything. For many years, when I was trying to find my

*A grateful heart
is a gift in itself.*

way in the world, if people asked me about my background, I would
say that my parents were working class. Both my parents did work very
hard, but the truth is we were definitely poor. No getting around that
hard fact, no matter how much I wanted to sugar coat the truth.

I was ashamed. I also resented the toil and hardship that my family went through trying to
make ends meet, while living in fear that the rent man would kick us out into the streets when
my parents got behind with the rent. I did not believe my dad when he said that there were
many people around the world worse off than us, and I did not care about starving children
in faraway Africa. Shabby hand-me-downs became my wardrobe staple, even as I fantasized
each night about owning a pair of hip new leather boots. It was these humbling childhood
conditions, however, that became the fertile ground for the gratefulness that has become a way
of life to me over the years.

You can choose gratitude

My childhood hardship brought with it the blessing of a deep appreciation for the simpler
things of life. To this day, it doesn't take much for me to be happy, and I can always find
something to be grateful for, no matter what's going on in my life. I enjoy the good life, but I
am not impressed by extravagance, and I am definitely turned off by greed. I have had money
and not had money, and had it again.

I would rather have than not, but I would not fall
apart if I were to lose what I have. I can live without
material comforts, but I cannot live without peace of

*If you only have one prayer
let it be the words, thank you.*

mind. It seems to me that whether we feel rich or poor depends more on our capacity for gratefulness than how much money we have in the bank. So much of what is beautiful and valuable in life is free anyway. You don't need a hefty financial portfolio to appreciate the splendor of a breathtaking golden orange sunset or the priceless clean slate of health after a lengthy illness.

> *Happiness cannot be traveled to, owned, earned, worn or consumed.*
> *Happiness is the spiritual experience of living every minute with*
> *love, grace and gratitude.*

—Denis Waitley

Gratitude is easy to come by when life is light and wonderful. It doesn't require much depth and insight to be grateful when all is going well for us. The deeper value and rewards come when we can experience gratitude even in the midst of challenge and uncertainty. Yes, there are times in all of our lives when we feel so weary and burdened by responsibilities and concerns that it's hard to feel grateful about much at all. Just making it through a day, or even an hour, can be a test of our resilience and emotional stamina.

At other times, it is very tempting to look at what we don't have instead of what we do. In our materialistic society, it is easy to get stuck in the demoralizing mindset of thinking the grass is always greener on the other side. Someone will inevitably seem better off than us. When we are hooked into this unrealistic illusion, it is hard to feel content and grateful for much of anything in our own seemingly inadequate lives.

You can always find something to complain about if that is what you are looking for. You can also choose to take the opposite approach. When you make a conscious decision to make gratitude a way of life, instead of a once a year remembrance, your life will be enriched beyond measure. Sometimes it takes a wake-up call to shake us out of our lethargy and sense of entitlement to remember that life itself is the greatest gift of all. When we, or a loved one, experience a serious illness, then nothing but life itself seems important. When my mum was edging close to death, seeing her smile and eat a little pureed food would make my day.

> *A thankful person is thankful under all circumstances.*
> *A complaining soul complains even if he is living in paradise.*

—Baha'u'llah

Clarity and perspective

Gratitude doesn't belittle our suffering, but it does help us to maintain a balanced perspective. I have learned that difficult times pass, and there is usually something good to be found in even the most trying of conditions. I am happiest when I choose to be grateful, instead of waiting for life to make me happy by turning out exactly the way I want, which it seldom does. Sometimes that is actually a very good thing, as many times I have been very pleasantly surprised that life turns out better than I expected.

I live by the old adage that *life usually turns out best for those who make the best of how life turns out.* I give thanks not only for all the blessings I already have, but also for all those that are yet to come. It's not Pollyanna or wishful thinking; I just know there is a very clear, tangible flow of positive energy that we set into motion when we make gratitude a way of life.

I give thanks in advance and then surrender the outcome to the Divine will. I expect good, but I am not attached to a specific outcome. I believe that if something belongs to me, it is bound to come to me. If not, as Rev. Michael Beckwith, founder and spiritual director of the Agape International Spiritual Center, often reminds his congregants, then it just didn't have my name on it. Life becomes a whole lot more easygoing living from this viewpoint. Acceptance is key, not coercion.

Give thanks for all that is and all that is yet to be.

We cannot force life to behave the way we want it to, but we can affect our response to life by our capacity for genuine, heartfelt gratefulness. When we relax and give thanks for what is, instead of living in a state of angst about our need for more, we actually open the way for greater good to enter into our lives. You can practice gratefulness by paying attention to all the good in your life from the moment you wake up until you go to sleep at night. Consider keeping a "gratitude journal," and each day write down the good things that happened to you, no matter how small and insignificant they may seem.

Service

God has no other hands than ours.
—Dorothy Solle

For me, gratitude and service go hand in hand. When thankfulness for all that we have been given becomes a way of life, compassion and the desire to serve others naturally follows. As we age, service to others brings greater meaning and purpose into our own lives. A life without service is unthinkable to me. Giving is not an obligatory act I do to compensate for my privileged life because I also know what it's like to struggle and go without.

Giving is one of life's greatest joys.

I give because it's a direct way to use my life in a manner that comforts and benefits others, which in turn brings more meaning, peace, and happiness back to me. Not all of us can give materially in such a grand manner like the remarkable Warren Buffet or Oprah. But we can, as Mother Teresa once said, do little things with great love.

And sometimes, it's the giving of ourselves, our company, and our time that holds more value than anything material. If you have money, use it well—tithe, donate, give—if you don't, there are numerous ways you can be of service to others. Everyone has some quality, talent, or gift that we can use to make a difference. A few years ago, I volunteered as a "cuddler" at the neonatal intensive care unit at the Los Angeles Children's Hospital.

It doesn't take much talent or skill to sit in a rocking chair holding a very sick baby in your arms for an afternoon, and I probably derived as much comfort out of it as hopefully the babies did. I met a darling older man at the hospital called Jim who was also a cuddler. He said it gave his life purpose now that he was retired, to come to the hospital everyday and hold a sick baby or read to a quarantined child who had leukemia.

> *One act of benificence, one act of real usefulness,*
> *is worth all the abstract sentiment in the world.*
>
> —Anne Radcliffe

Over the years, I have participated in all kinds of volunteering, from working as a docent at the Simon Wiesenthal Museum of Tolerance to delivering food to the homes of people with AIDS. Sometimes it has been pleasurable, other times challenging, but always rewarding. Without exception, I have come away with the sense that my life had been enriched because of it. I learned about the amazing strength and resilience of the human spirit in the face of adversity.

I also learned, for reasons I frequently do not understand, that from birth until death, suffering is a part of life. Why that is, I do not have the answer. What I do know is that each one of us can do something to try to alleviate the conditions that create suffering, whether it is close to home or in a faraway distant country.

When we are kind to someone, they might be more inclined to be kind to the next person they encounter and so on.

There are moments in life when we look at the world and all the suffering and wonder how anything we do can ever make a difference. But we can and we do. We give and facilitate change through our political involvement, our money, our time, and more importantly our enthusiastic commitment to those who need our help.

I have deep admiration and respect for the many people who adopt multiple children without the financial resources that most celebrities who adopt are fortunate to have. My husband Alan has been a long time Big Brother to a boy called Ben. Ben has seven siblings who are all adopted like him by two sisters who decided to use their lives to give children from disadvantaged backgrounds a loving family.

Sometimes when I hear stories like this, a part of me feels bad that I don't have it in me to give like that. I hear about women volunteering for the Peace Corps in some third world country or enlisting to serve with an organization like Doctors Without Borders, and I am humbled and inspired at the same time.

Practice random acts of kindness

Everyday we can affect the lives of others by what may seem like the smallest thing, and we each hold the potential to ease human suffering in some way. A warm smile, a sincere thank you to a sales person who waited on you, a few reassuring words of support for someone who is going through a difficult time, or perhaps a moment to listen to a stranger might be the most perfect and timely gift you could give. Sometimes, it is the small kindnesses that sustain us the most.

Americans, for the most part, love to give. Many of us give generously and without hesitation whenever we can. Yesterday I watched an edition of the Oprah show that featured ordinary Americans using their lives in unique and extraordinary ways. One woman said that she felt called to do something to help children, so she came up with a plan to provide sleepwear for kids.

These were kids who, more often than not, went to sleep in the only clothes they had, the ones on their backs. A simple idea really, but through her concerned efforts, she was able to come up with almost one hundred thousand sets of sleepwear for some needy and well-deserving youngsters.

Be kind in all you say and do
because acts of kindness follow you.
With just one kindness a chain will start
to grow and glow from heart to heart.
—Anonymous

Do our donations really help?

Sometimes, however, people question if their donations ever reach those they hope to help, and even if it does, they wonder if their $15, $25, or $75 donations can actually make a crucial difference in other people's lives. Well, in answer to that, I came upon this information obtained from Oprah's Angel Network and *O* magazine. Here's an example of three remarkable charities and how your money can be used, as researched and presented by her Angel Network team:

- At **Free The Children** (freethechildren.org), your $15 donation can provide a poor

Chinese child with a school kit that includes a year's worth of supplies—notebooks, pencils, erasers, crayons, a book bag, and more.

- At **America's Second Harvest** (secondharvest.org), your $25 donation guarantees that five hundred pounds of groceries will be allotted to soup kitchens, food pantries, churches, women's shelters, after school programs, and community kitchens across America.

- At **Women For Women International** (womenforwomen.org), your $75 donation purchases a knitting machine and vocational skills training for a Rwandan woman, who can then create an income by selling the clothing she produces. Like me, you can become a sponsor and give financial aid and emotional support to one woman. One of the things I love about being a monthly sponsor is my "sister" and I get to exchange letters. For a woman who may have lost everything, letters of support help renew her hope for a better future. Just $27 a month (for many of us, the cost of a week's supply of a Starbucks mocha soy latte) allows women in war torn regions of the world to obtain basic necessities for their families like food, clean water, medicine, or school books for their children—things we take for granted in America.

Be kind for everyone you meet is fighting their greatest battle.

—Plato

Inspiration is all around us

I am inspired by the many different ways in which people I admire give, and then I do what works for me. Some of the people I admire are well known, but most are not. All of them use their lives to make a difference to the world in which they live. And sometimes I get inspiration from strangers. Today I witnessed this loving act of random kindness. At the entrance to my local Whole Foods market, I watched a young man approach an older man who was soliciting money for a homeless shelter. I don't know how much money the young man gave, if any, but I do know that he treated the older man with a kindness and respect that was beautiful to see.

He asked the man if he was hungry and thirsty, and out of his grocery bag he handed him an apple and a bottle of juice. Not much really, certainly not costly, but a sweet act of loving kindness that I could tell by the surprised happy look on the older man's face was unexpected and deeply appreciated.

There are moments in our lives when we have time and energy to volunteer, and times when writing a check for a worthwhile cause is the best we can do.

And yes, sometimes it is hard to muster up compassion for others when we are entrenched in difficult times ourselves. At such times, however, I have found that acknowledging my own challenges have made me more conscious and sensitive to the challenges and suffering that we all experience as a part of our collective human experience. Our suffering may be different—a woman in India who struggles to support her family on a dollar a day can hardly have compassion for a well-off American woman whose biggest concern of the day may be smooth skin and being cellulite free.

Then again, who are we to judge one another? That same American woman may, in fact, dedicate her life to helping others, even as she splurges on her miracle creams. Still, I am vastly aware that the challenges I have experienced in my life can never compare to the insurmountable hardships and struggles that many people on our planet endure every single day.

We can all be a hero to someone

During the two years before my mum died, Dad took care of her around the clock pretty much by himself. Though he collapsed exhausted into bed every night, he wouldn't have had it any other way. Dad knew how important it was for her to look her best, no matter how sick she was. Every night while he bathed her, he would gently shave the hair above her mouth and on her chin. Then he would dress her in one of her favorite nightgowns before he settled her into bed for their nightly prayers.

I watched him do this when I visited home, and I always cried as I witnessed the exquisite gift of love in action that Dad gave to Mum. No, not the romantic kind of love. Taking care of a sick and dying spouse is never romantic or easy, which makes the memory of it so valuable and unforgettable to me. When I mentioned to him how grateful I was for all his caring and giving, he responded by saying that's just what we do. We love and we give without fuss.

Every day all over the world, that's what people do; they give in quiet selfless ways just like my dad, or Ben's mom and her sister, or my friend Joe at the children's hospital. They don't get the big headlines or the awards, but they are the heroes. We serve in the ways we can for as long as we can, because, after all, that's what being human is all about.

May all beings be free from pain and suffering,
may all beings be at peace.
—Buddha

LOVE

One word frees us from all the weight and pain of life.
That word is Love.

—Sophocles

There is one essential that no human being can live without at any stage in life, and that essential is love. We spend much of our life yearning for more love and deeper intimacy with others. We're happy when we have love and miserable without it. I have found that love is a lot like joy. We need both to live fully and age well. As we age, connection with others is vital to our longevity and health. Without it, we feel secluded and disconnected from the world.

Lack of connection and familial support can bring depression and illness, and studies have shown that having a supportive network of people who love and care for us can even lower blood pressure and reduce the risk of Alzheimer's disease. We need each other to make sense of our place in the world and to draw strength from in times of need.

Online chatting may be fun and harmless in small doses, but not at the expense of intimacy with those we live.

In today's high-tech world, especially in American, many people spend too much time talking online instead of connecting with people in person—and that can be a problem. Online chat rooms are a beneficial way to connect with others for those who, for various reasons, are housebound. For the rest of us, if we are addicted to the seduction of endless talking to strangers online, rather than with those whom we share our daily lives, you might want to ask yourself why.

Three's company

Make yourself necessary to someone.

—Ralph Waldo Emerson

My family, especially Alan and Arielle, are my safe sanctuary in an often cold and uncaring world. A few months ago, I was feeling particularly overwhelmed, and my energy and spirits were low. My dog had recently died, we'd had a lot of company staying with us, and a work project was stressing me out big time.

One afternoon, I went into the bedroom where Alan was quietly reading the newspaper. I lay down next to him, said nothing, and burst out crying. Loud heaving sobs poured out of me as I curled up in his arms. He didn't need to ask what was wrong; he already knew. Arielle was in her room, and she heard me crying and came into our bedroom. She lay next to me and wrapped her arms around me, and she too said nothing. We lay there, the three of us, me howling like a mad woman, while they silently, and with great tenderness and understanding, cradled me in their loving arms until my weeping subsided.

A few days ago, I was able to reciprocate some of that love back to Arielle. She was feeling low and weary and asked if I'd lie down and take a nap with her before she had to go to work. She said that lying in her mama's arms always helps her fall asleep when she is troubled. I got into bed with her as I have done so many times before, and held her in my arms and stroked her head while she slept.

I didn't sleep. I didn't want to miss out on the joy I was feeling in that moment. I dozed a little, but mostly just gazed out of the window thinking how incredibly blessed I am to still get the chance to comfort her in such a way.

The three of us have always been exceptionally close and delighted in each other's company. When I have good news, they are the ones I want to celebrate with first. When I feel small and insignificant to the world, they help me feel huge with possibilities again. I have learned how to soothe and comfort myself emotionally, but the love that we share as a family is invaluable to me as it is to them. We all need a sense of belonging and of being necessary, even if it's just to one other person. I feel tremendously fortunate that I have two. To this day, the sweetest words in the world to me are the words, "I love you, Mama." I am happy to say I hear them often.

Family

Call it a clan, call it a network, call it a tribe, call it a family.
Whatever you call it, whoever you are, you need one.

—Jane Howard

I left England to live in Japan when I was seventeen, so my parents got used to me being far away from home. I missed them, but like many young people, I was focused on my life and career. I had no desire to stay in Yorkshire, nor did they want that for me. They wanted me to have what they never had and supported me all the way.

I always knew that travel would be a huge part of my life, and one of the perks my global trotting was that my parents got to visit me in Japan and then frequently in Los Angeles. When I became a mother, I felt a greater need to be closer to them. I saw their aging, and I began to understand how little time we have together on this journey through life.

During the last ten years of my mum's life, I spent as much time with her as I could, but I always felt it was never enough. When her health began to severely deteriorate, the worry and stress of being so far away from both of them kept me awake many a night. Fortunately, my brother lived close by, and my parents had a solid network of supportive friends and

We need loving family, friends, and community to give meaning to our existence.

neighbors to help them out. It was not, however, a replacement for their eldest daughter being there to assist and comfort them. The care of both my parents became my greatest daily concern.

As it turned out, I was soon given the gift of being my dad's caretaker as he recuperated from a high risk, emergency heart surgery. After much persuasion, I had finally convinced my dad to come to L.A. for Arielle's high school graduation. I was so happy to have him with us, but from the moment he arrived, it became clear that the stress of taking care of Mum was taking a heavy toll on him. He had been with us only five days when we discovered that he needed an immediate quadruple bypass, or we could lose him any day. Apparently he was a walking miracle.

I shudder at the thought that his heart could have conked out on the long flight over. A three-week visit turned into a three-month rehabilitation, and caring for his every need became the purpose and joy of my life during that time. As I cared for him, my dad and I shared an intimacy much deeper than ever before. Our daily walks and picnics on the beach were highlights of the long summer days and weeks together. Though he made a full recovery in those three months, my mum died a week after his return to England.

In my heart, I believe that she waited until he was well enough to return home. While I wish I had more time with my mum in the end, I have had no unfinished business or unresolved issues with either of my parents. For this, I am deeply grateful.

Intimacy requires courage because risk is inescapable.

—Rollo May

Arielle has mentioned on many occasions that she does not want to live far away from her dad and I when she is married and has children of her own. We couldn't agree more. Arielle and I share the same spirit of independence and adventure, but I am glad that she wants to live as close to us as she can. Her dad and I don't want to miss out on any moment when we become grandparents. I never knew any of my grandparents, unlike Alan who spent his childhood living with both sets of grandparents in a three-story family home in New Jersey. He recalls that the noise level was intense at times with two rival grandmas, but the food was always outstanding, as Becky and Dora tried to outdo each other over latkes and matzo ball soup.

Two English mums

Two years after Mum died, my dad remarried a wonderful woman called Jean. A few months before Mum died, Jean's husband also died after a lengthy battle with cancer. Jean and her husband had been longtime friends with my parents since they were all in their twenties, so it's a lovely turn of fate that Dad and Jean ended up together after such a long history. They are a source of comfort and companionship for each other, and I couldn't be happier for them.

I had a very special moment with Jean during my last visit to England. One night after dinner, my dad played me a tape recording Alan had made over fifteen years ago of my mum, Arielle, and I singing. I had completely forgotten that night years ago in Alan's studio when we were all singing, laughing and having a really good time. It was so sweet to hear a very young and exuberant Arielle belt out her favorite Disney songs, and I didn't even mind my seriously off pitch but spirited attempt at "Edelweiss" from *The Sound Of Music*. But it was hearing the lovely voice of my mum sing "I Could Have Danced All Night" that literally took my breath away.

It had been ages since I had heard my mum's singing voice, and it was the first time since her death four years ago that I heard her speak. In that moment, I went from light-hearted laughter to uncontrollable sobs. Jean was sitting next to me, put her arms around me, and held me close to her ample bosom just as Mum used to do. "Go on love," she said in her broad Yorkshire accent I love so much, "we all need to have a good cry now and again." I stayed like that in her arms for quite a while, feeling happy and sad, but mostly grateful that I've had the good fortune of not just one, but two loving English mums in this lifetime.

Happiness is having a large, loving, close-knit family,
far away in another city.

—George Burns

Caring for our elders

One of the things I always admired about the Japanese culture is the way they honor their elders. There is a reverence and respect that is sadly missing here in America, where old age is more likely to be considered a burden than an asset. In Japan, they even have a designated Respect the Elderly day. In India, the older you are, the more advice and council is sought. In a remote section of Alaska, the Inuit elders are considered the most valuable members of their community.

Many elderly people in this country grew up in a communal environment surrounded by family and relatives. But in their old age and in time of greatest need, many folks find themselves alone and isolated, apart from the company of hired help.

Social isolation like this can lead to depression and is often the cause behind seniors' suicide. According to the National Council on Aging, suicides and murder-suicides involving elderly individuals and couples are rising at an alarming rate. Last week, I read in the newspaper about an elderly man who was found dead in his apartment six months after he had died. Apparently he was a surly, widowed chap and estranged from his only adult child. I don't know how he lived his life, but no one should have to die so alone and uncared for like that. It's just too sad. The Beatles' song "Eleanor Rigby" makes me want to cry when I think about all the lonely people out there in the world, especially the elderly.

> *People should not have to endure old age, illness, and death in isolation: we all need someone we can turn to.*

Intergenerational living is a thing of the past for most people. A sad fact when each generation has something special and unique to offer the other. There are many children who are lonely and neglected, just as there are seniors who haven't held a baby or hugged a child in years.

I love the concept of communities and diverse communes of people of all generations coming together to make the journey through life a little easier. Such communities exist all over the country, many in places like Berkeley, California, and at the Hope Meadows community in Illinois.

If Alan were to die first, I can imagine myself in my elderly years being quite happy in a community of this sort. Having the privacy of my own room and then coming together with others young and old to share a meal and interesting conversation appeals to me. Of course, Arielle says the guesthouse at her future, Spanish-style estate (she has big dreams) is where she expects me to spend my twilight years. I think I'll choose the latter.

Remembering Violet

One thing that became clear to me as both a volunteer at a nursing home and as a cuddler at the children's hospital is that from birth until death, we all need the healing comfort of human touch. Rocking a sick infant or holding the hand of a lonely elderly woman who has cancer is really all the same. We all need to be loved and cared for. I often think about the lovely elder woman named Violet who I met at the hospital where Mum spent her last days.

Violet was dying of cancer, and she rarely had visitors. One day while my dad attempted to feed Mum her pureed food, I decided to see if Violet would like my help in feeding her. Instead, she reached for my hand, and with a despondent glaze in her sad, blue eyes she looked deep into me and asked, "What are we supposed to do? What does God want us to do?"

I will never forget her words or the look in her eyes. I did not have an answer for her then, and I don't really think she was looking for one. Sometimes, especially during those difficult years of many personal losses, I felt as confused and uncertain as she was. What I did know and understand was to be present with her in that moment without the need to give her a trite answer or an attempt to take away her sadness.

Love stretches your heart and makes you big inside.

—Margaret Walker

I held her hand and very tenderly stroked her hair. Tears fell down her face, and with all the love in my heart I whispered, "I don't know, Violet. I really don't know." She squeezed my hand, and we sat together in silence and not knowing, and at that moment I felt a gentle peace wash over us both.

Since that moment four years ago, I have pondered Violet's question many times. I always come back to this—what we are supposed to do? What I believe God really wants us to do is just love each other. Love can melt away all pain and give us hope. I wish I could have told Violet this. Maybe it was too late in life, and she was just too sad and lonely to have believed it anyway.

Stay connected

I love that when Arielle was in college, she and my dad wrote letters to each other, sharing what was going on in each of their lives. My dad is the only grandparent that Arielle has, so he is extra cherished by all of us. Our children watch how we treat our parents, and in a way we are teaching them how to treat us when we become elders. One of the things I noticed and appreciated about Alan when we first met was how dedicated and loving he was with his mom. Not in one of those strange, Freudian Oedipal sort of ways, but in a sweet, good Jewish son kind of way. It says a lot about a man how he is with his mother.

Let parents then bequeath to their children
not riches but the spirit of reverence.

—Plato

I am closer to my brother and sister now than ever before, even though geographically we all still live a great distance apart. My mum's death and my dad's heart surgery brought us all closer together. I visit my dad and brother in England every year and love having them, my sister, and her family stay with us in Los Angeles. It doesn't take much time and effort to stay connected, just the willingness and intention to do so.

I call my dad and brother every week, speak to my sister in Michigan a couple of times a week, and e-mail in between. My sister's family and my clan also do video cam get-togethers now and again as a way to see each other while we talk and catch up. I also try and practice the lost art of handwritten letters on beautiful stationary whenever I can. I love it when I unexpectedly receive a handwritten letter or card in the mail, instead of all the bills and junk mail.

We may not get to choose all our family members, but we do get to choose our friends and that includes our canine pals. They get all excited when we come home after a long day and love us even when we're grouchy. How many humans would do that for you?

Our loved ones are only a call or e-mail away, no matter how far apart we may live.

Puppy love

My little dog—a heart beat at my feet.

—Edith Wharton

We all know that dogs make great loyal companions, but they also help to lower our blood pressure, keep us active, and fend off depression. They help us live longer and better; they bring out the goodness in us and accept us the way we are. If we treat them well, they will love us unconditionally. They ask little of us, really, but give back so much.

Six months ago my beloved sixteen-year-old dog Whiskey died. This is what I know; it hurt as much as I imagined. Worse actually. Making the decision to end his life was one of the hardest things I have ever done, even though I had no doubt it was the only thing to do. I still miss him so much; it feels like a jab in my heart. Over the last four years with Arielle away at college and Alan on tour, he became my constant companion. Every night he slept on the bed next to me snuggled up as close as he could get, and we became completely in sync with each other's daily routines.

When my mum passed away, there was a terrible sadness, but somehow her death made sense. She had been sick for too long, and her death felt like a merciful relief for her and for us. It felt different with Whiskey. Some of you will understand this, and some will think I have lost my marbles. I did not grow up with pets, so I had no idea it was possible to love and miss a dog this deeply.

Is it mere coincidence that the word DOG is actually GOD spelled backwards?

Despite being sixteen, his illness snuck up on us and caught the three of us off guard. This past year, I began to notice his aging just as much as my own. His spine was out of alignment, causing him back pain, and he recently developed a severe case of pancreatitis and a stubborn urinary infection. Whiskey was a fluffy, white, eleven-pound Maltese-Bichon mix of absolute joy. Because he was a small dog, we were told that he could possibly live till he was twenty-one or twenty-two. We thought we might have another four or five years left with him.

We were wrong. This sweet little bundle of pure love brought each of us so much happiness that it is a very hard fact to accept that he is gone. I see him everywhere around the house and on the street outside—sleeping on his favorite spot on the master bed, or running home on the last leg of his walk in anticipation of food. Like all dogs, he loved to eat, but would not take a morsel of food in the last few days. It broke my heart.

A love magnet

I loved Whiskey more than I can explain in words. Sometimes I would love to bury my face in his soft fur and breathe in his warm doggy smell. He knew when I was having a bad day, as he seemed to snuggle up even closer. When I cried, he would look deeply at me with his soulful eyes and twitch his eyebrows one at a time as if in a sympathetic, understanding nod. I think he got a bit impatient with me when I would slobber kisses all over him, but I couldn't help myself. He was an irresistible love magnet and oozed love through every pore.

As most dog lovers will tell you, a dog is not just a dog. Whiskey was a cherished member of our family—how do you put a price tag on that? People without dogs think we dog lovers are a bit indulgent and a tad insane in the way we lavish our dogs with such adoration. What do they know?

Americans love dogs, and according to the American Pet Products Manufactures Association, there are 74.8 million pet dogs in this country, and the average cost of a dog is $331. Overall, dogs in this country have it pretty good, but not as good as dogs in France. We may have doggie parks and doggie day spas, but so far American dogs are not allowed to join their owners for dinner in a nice bistro or café like those lucky French pooches do. On the other hand, American dogs don't end up on the dinner table as they often do in China. So count ours lucky.

Studies show that pets and especially dogs are good for our health.

As for people who are cruel to animals, they are as despicable to me as Anne Coulter and Dick Cheney. If I had the resources, I would adopt as many abandoned dogs as I could. Arielle already has her own future plan set in mind. Along with the guesthouse where Alan and I are apparently going to live one day, she is also going to buy a huge piece of land and call it Doggie Heaven. The name speaks for itself.

You think dogs will not be in heaven? I tell you they will be there long before any of us.

—Robert Louis Stevenson

There's something about dogs that can bring a grown man to his knees crying. I've seen it in my husband, and I shudder to think how my strapping brother will cope when his best buddy Josh—a beautiful golden lab—is gone. Man, woman, or child, there's nothing quite like losing these special friends.

When Whiskey was well, he would, on occasion, sit on my lap and let me pet him for a short while. Then he'd soon jump up and be off to play or check out what was happening in another part of the house. The days leading up to his passing, however, when he was so sick I knew euthanasia was inevitable, he would sit and melt into my lap for the longest time. Even when my leg went numb, I would not move because I knew our time together was short, and I did not want that moment to end. I was very conscious of every ticking moment that brought us closer to losing him. The moment just before Whiskey died, he looked directly and deeply at both Arielle and I as if to say, *it's okay, it's time for me to go now. It's been grand, but I've had enough.*

Every morning, Whiskey would wake Alan and I up with a wet lick and a nudge to get out of bed and walk and feed him. I miss that terribly, but we are not ready to open up our hearts and home to another dog just yet. In time we will, but he is a hard act to follow. For the first time in eighteen years, we do not have a dog. It feels strange at times, but for now we are also enjoying the space and treasured memories.

Whiskey may be physically gone from our lives, but the love we shared over the years will remain a constant. He was a gift that kept on giving, and one we will never forget. We held a memorial service for Whiskey with a group of our dog-loving friends, and shared stories and photos of him to celebrate his life.

Though death and loss are never easy, passing is an opportunity to show appreciation and celebrate a life, instead of just mourning a loss. We are conditioned to laugh when a baby is born, but cry when our loved ones die. Maybe death is also a time of celebration—a celebration of a life well lived and anticipation of what is yet to come.

There is no psychiatrist in the world like a puppy licking your face.

—Ben Williams

Celebrations

I love celebrations, especially ones that involve food. Food is a big part of celebration for most people, and most definitely so in my family. We love to eat and eat well. Is there anything better than sitting around a table with dear friends sharing stories and catching up over good food?

My friend Adrienne makes a divine traditional English Christmas feast that I look forward to for months. With fluffy Yorkshire pudding that is as good as my dad's, killer mince pies that are not too sweet, and sherry trifle with a hint of brandy that you cannot do justice to with only one helping. Every year since our girls were in preschool together, Adrienne and I have celebrated Christmas with my family, her husband Jeff, and daughter Lina. We don't see as much of each other as we'd like throughout the year, but we know that on that one special day each year, we will come together once more to enjoy that long family tradition.

For years we have celebrated the Jewish holidays with our dear friends, Meredith and Nicole, and enjoy the yummiest potato latkes that Nicole and Arielle spend all day making from scratch. The four of us would also take turns on making dinner while we watched the Academy Awards or the Golden Globes. Since Meredith recently married, the Jewish holiday dinners have grown more elaborate and fun, as her husband Mitch has a big family and also a wicked sense of humor. Thanksgiving dinner and Christmas Eve are celebrated with Debbie, Phil, and their clan. If we're lucky to be graced with her presence, this gathering will include Debbie's delightful Italian mom, Emily.

You can dream up your own reasons to celebrate and come together with friends and loved ones. Celebrate a full moon, moving to a new home, or the summer solstice. Have a soiree to celebrate spring fever and the joy of being alive. Celebrate a special anniversary, becoming newly single, a new job, or the completion of a successful project. Host a salon at your home where friends gather to enjoy hors d'oeuvres, a glass of wine, and share a creative art form. At one salon I attended, someone read a poem they had written, another person presented photos they had taken for an exhibit, while one woman did a fascinating performance piece of interpretive dance that included sign language.

We don't have to wait for a particular occasion or holy day to celebrate life.

RELATIONSHIPS

Imagine that every person in the world is enlightened but you.
They are all your teachers, each doing the right things to help
you learn perfect patience, perfect wisdom and perfect compassion.

—Buddha

Relationship is the most powerful tool for growth and transformation—it is also one of the most difficult. As we age, there is generally an increased desire for healthier relationships and less time and energy to squander on those that are not. Reaching this place of awareness starts with a lot of soul searching and introspection. It has taken much time and self-induced anguish for me to understand that in order for any of my relationships to work, I have to work on myself first.

The moment we start taking responsibility for our own thoughts and behaviors, we stop projecting our unrealistic needs and expectations on to others. Not an easy place to get to, but highly rewarding when we see what a difference it makes in the quality of our relationships, and more importantly, in the quality of our own emotional wellness. Here is some of what I have learned, from friendships to marriage, and what I try and remember when I still get stuck.

Girlfriends

Getting together with my girlfriends is a priority, even though we all live full very busy lives. I love the laughter, support, and honesty that I share with them. I don't have long lists of girlfriends (don't have the time or the need), but the ones I do have are very special to me. I have women that I connect with only now and again with an occasional phone call or e-mail, and others I may have lunch with a few times a year.

Then there is what I call my inner circle of a few wonderful women who I see often, and that includes my dear friend Debbie who is like family to me and talk to most days. Debbie is Italian, very warm and friendly, and makes the best eggplant parmesan you'll ever taste. Unlike me, she is a *people person* and a generous networker. We've been close friends for about five years, but it feels like we've been friends for lifetimes. My friend Pam has a very sweet, compassionate nature, a lovely singing voice, and a killer whistle, which makes her great to have around at concerts.

Women have come and gone in my life for various reasons. I've lived in three different countries, and in the past wasn't very good at keeping in touch once I moved away. I can also be a bit of a loner at times. It's just my nature, but the older I get the more effort I put into nurturing my established friendships and opening myself up to new ones. Some friends have left my life for reasons of their own, or we just grew apart. Others, I made a conscious decision to let go of because I have no space in my life for unhealthy relationships.

"Good friends are like stars ... You don't always see them, but you know they are always there.

—Anonymous

Moving on

I know from personal experience that when a long-time friend goes against us, it can be a devastating blow. I also know that once the fire of my anger has cooled down, and I am able to detach myself from the drama a bit, most of the time I have found that it all worked out for the best.

When misunderstandings, envy, and resentments begin to poison a relationship, the healthiest and most loving thing we can do is to let them go and move on. I know things are not always equal in our relationships, and we all have different things we are working on. I also know it is hard to wish others well when we are hurting and lacking in our own lives. I am not, however, willing to play small so another can feel better about herself. It's not healthy for either of us, and it's not the kind of friendship I am interested in. We may not get to choose our next of kin, but we do get to choose our friends.

I am happy to say that my inner circle of friends are as supportive and encouraging about what I am going for in my life as I am for them. I value honesty and integrity in myself and my friends, and that is not possible when someone is outwardly expressing affection while seething with resentment underneath. That said, I am willing to give my friends some necessary slack, as I'm sure they do for me, because we all screw up and fall short now and again.

The end of a friendship can be a painful thing to endure when two women were once very close.

Many women are not great at confrontation, myself included. But I have learned that if something is really bothering me in a relationship, it's much healthier to say what needs to be said in a direct but non-attacking manner, or get over it in my own head. In order for me to move on, I allow myself time to grieve my loss, and then I consciously send love to my ex-friend through my thoughts and prayers. By letting go of any residue resentment, I am able to soothe my heart and restore peace to my once troubled mind.

I have come to believe ... that what is most important to me must be spoken, made verbal and shared, even at the risk of having it bruised or misunderstood.

—Audre Lorde

Girl talk

Girlfriends get to do that special nurturing kind of talk that women are so good at. For many, they fill the emotional gaps that often exist in marriage and family, and help us remember who we really are outside of those roles that we play in the world. And yet despite this, many women get overly busy with work and family, setting friendships with other women aside. Not a good thing.

Once our children are off to college, it often leaves a noticeable gap within ourselves and a longing for the kind of emotional closeness and support that only women can give to each other. The good news is that we can develop new friendships at any stage in our lives and revitalize ones that we have let fall by the wayside. All it takes is your intention and receptivity; then you may be pleasantly surprised at the wonderful amazing women you start to draw into your life.

Every now and again I give myself a reminder to check in with friends I haven't connected with in a while. Sometimes it's just a quick e-mail asking how they are and that I was thinking about them. Other times, I take out my phone book and call friends as near and far away as Japan just to say hello. My friend Debbie's husband Phil is also a very dear friend, which allows for fun double dating. Alan and I have a number of other special couples that we enjoy spending time with—Pam and John, Cheryl and Steven, Meredith and Mitch to name a few.

There is no replacement for girlfriends, no matter how close we might be to our romantic partners.

Getting together with just the women is a whole other trip. The conversation is effortlessly deep and profound, then light and deliciously wicked in a fashion only we women are expert at. Last summer, Debbie, Pam, and I started a weekly ritual of getting together every Monday for an afternoon picnic at the beach. And when Alan or Phil are out of town, the three of us get together for a girl's night of sushi, face masks, and lots of laughs. Who says you can't have raucous sleepovers at fifty?

An antidote to stress

I get by with a little help from my friends.

—John Lennon

Arielle recently sent me an e-mail concerning a landmark UCLA study on friendship amongst women. Scientists now suspect that spending time with good friends can actually reduce the kind of stress most of us experience on a daily basis. This famed Nurses' Study from Harvard Medical School found that the more friends women have, the less likely they are to develop physical impairments as they age, and the more likely they are to lead a joyful life.

In fact, the results were so significant, the researchers concluded, that not having close friends or confidantes were as detrimental to your health as smoking or carrying extra weight. While it's nice to have a scientific study validate spending time with our women friends, we all know that it just feels great and comforting, and that's all we really need to know.

If you are looking to make new friends, you could join a women's group, a book club, or your local yoga studio. Pick up a copy of your neighborhood newspaper or brochures and check the community bulletins in cafés, markets, and your favorite bookstore. Volunteer for a day of service at a church or animal shelter; you never know who you might meet.

Can't we all just get along?

All people and relationships come into our lives for a reason. That reason, first and foremost, is to learn something about ourselves. Sometimes, that will be an easygoing beautiful thing. More often than not, however, it will be a gigantic hurdle that will knock the wind out of us from time to time. We draw certain people into our lives whose sole purpose is to serve as a mirror for the things we need to change about ourselves. I have learned that these relationships are the most prized and valuable. I have probably grown more

If you think that someone else is always the problem then that mode of thinking is the problem itself.

from the harsh wounds of betrayal than I have from the comfort of soothing love and support. I would not have believed this at the time, of course. Sometimes those we love the most—spouse, parents, children—may also turn out to be the biggest button pushers of all time (we will thank them for this one day).

Taking responsibility is tough for most of us to accept. It is much easier and satisfying on some level to blame others. You can try and skirt your way around this all you want. You can come up with endless reasons to justify why *they* are always wrong and not you. The same issues will keep showing up in the guise of different people until we figure out that it is we who have to stop reacting the same old way if we want different results. My girlfriend Molly describes it this way. You can put a paper bag over someone's head and keep going through the same painful stuff over and over until the light bulb goes on, and you finally get that it's all about you, not them.

Blame and judgment usually arise when a need or desire has not been met. Ah, expectations, the trap we all inevitably fall into—the *you did something for me so I expect something back in return* thing. We may not verbalize it that way or even consciously get that that's the game we're up to, but trust me, we are.

If you could read the secret history of your enemies,
we should see in each person's life, sorrow and suffering enough
to disarm all hostility.

—Longfellow

We all suffer and go through many of the same struggles, but we can never know the deeply rooted reasons, motives, or karma why people behave the way they do. Or, for instance, why they attract certain conditions and challenges to them. We're all on the same journey and will get to where we're going when we can. Our place is not to assume, judge, or even offer advice unless asked. Underneath all our surface differences and personal histories, we're all quite similar. We all want to be happy and loved. I am able to have greater understanding and compassion for others when I remember this truth.

If I want to attract loving relationships into my life, I have to be that love. If I want more understanding and compassion, I have to mirror those same qualities.

And then there's the really big thing that has helped me a lot. I try not to make assumptions about what I think others are thinking, especially in regards to me. Most of the time, as shocking as that might be for me to grasp, the humbling reality is that people are not thinking about me to the degree that I think they are, if at all. Whew, what a relief. Yes, you can now relax.

The other part that usually goes along with this is to refrain from personalizing. Most of the time a person's behavior is more about them than you. And if it's not, I'm sure they'll let you in on that, sooner rather than later.

The purpose of relationship is not happiness, but transformation.

—Andrew Schneider

MARRIAGE

I marry you, morning by morning, day by day, night by night ...

—John Ciardi

Now, if you really want to put into practice some of your hard-earned skills and wisdom, then let's talk about marriage. The one relationship where I can promise from extensive personal experience, you will be tested and rewarded more than any other.

Feeling beautiful at any age depends to a large degree on the quality of our relationships—with marriage being the most significant for many women. The person we choose to be our

That two people can share a life-long commitment to each other is a rare and astonishing thing.

marriage partner can have a profound affect on our health and aging. A healthy marriage can add years to your life, while a dysfunctional marriage can make you feel old before your time. Also, it seems to me that a woman who has been fully loved and treasured doesn't mourn the passing of her youth as much as one who has not.

At midlife, you may be enjoying the fruits of a long and mostly happy marriage, or you may be in the midst of ending a marriage that, for a variety of reasons, no longer serves your highest good. Wherever you may be on this spectrum, marriage for men and women alike remains one of the great enigmas, desires, and baffling challenges of life.

This year, Alan and I celebrated our twenty-eighth wedding anniversary. Quite an accomplishment if I may say so myself. Of course, I can't take all the credit. It takes two highly committed, constantly evolving individuals to make a marriage work. Even then, the odds are stacked against it. It's amazing to me that people make marriage work at all because it's not easy. Then again, nothing worthwhile usually is.

A mystery

What keeps some people together, while others can barely make it past the nuptials?

A successful marriage is a mystery—a rather lovely one, but a mystery nonetheless. There is no simple recipe for success that will suit all couples. Some people are simply not marriage material. That is not a judgment, just an observation. And sometimes a marriage may thrive despite all odds. When Alan and I first married, I had no long-term vision of how well we would do or how long we would last. I'd already been married once, so I didn't have a great track record. We went with it a day at a time, doing the best we could, and weathering the storms and frustrations and rejoicing in the grace and blessings.

I do know this: you will need stamina—this I can promise—and once again, an unflinching ability to look inward at yourself. Marriage has the potential to bring out the best and worst in us. Our personal growth will accelerate leaps and bounds though often against our own will. Sometimes, we will be tested to the point of sheer and complete exhaustion. Masks come off, and it's not always pretty and polite what's underneath. It's intense work that is not for the faint of heart. We have to get naked—and not just without clothes.

In a time when nothing is more certain than change,
the commitment of two people to one another has become difficult and rare.
Yet, by its scarcity, the beauty and value of this exchange have only been enhanced.

—Robert Sexton

Getting real

In marriage, there's no hiding our darkness and ugliness from each other, but that's when we have the chance to get real and grow up. This can only happen when there is a feeling of safety that comes from deep mutual trust and respect. In this protected space, we are free to be vulnerable and say the things that are hard to say to each other. Alan and I speak our truth even when it is difficult for the other to hear. We are not one of those couples who never argue (do they really exist?).

On the wrong day, I can have a fiery temper, and when provoked, so can he. But neither of us, even in the most volatile of moments, degrade our marriage and each other by lashing out cruel nastiness that cannot be taken back. This respect is part of why our love has endured. We know from experience that when an argument is getting way too overheated with no resolution in sight, we need some breathing space. One of us will usually leave for a while, or if it is late at night, we may sleep in separate bedrooms.

This is not a big deal to us. It is the healthy choice when words get in the way, and we are both exasperated and exhausted. Because we have a long history together and know how good we really have it, neither of us feels threatened by this. We know the importance of giving each other space to let the fire calm down so we can talk without shouting. We rarely wake up the

Researchers say that a good way to predict which couples will stay together over the long haul is to watch how they argue.

next morning without a renewed willingness on both our parts to make up. More often than not, the healing begins with a tentative embrace and the simple words *it's a new day, a new*

135

beginning. These words have become a kind of mantra that helps steer us through life and navigate through the challenges of marriage.

Sometimes, when I am really mad, Alan will point out that I foam at the mouth like a deranged dog. I do this—I must admit—and it is not attractive at all. Of course, when he tells me this in the heat of the moment, I get even madder. Then, despite myself, I usually burst into nervous laughter. Or maybe it's a laughing/crying thing. Either way, it usually eases the tension and helps us both lighten up a bit.

Successful couples, research shows, bring up problems in a constructive manner, keep strong emotions in check, and avoid disgust and contempt. According to Dr. Robert W. Levenson, director of the Institute of Personality and Social Research at the University of California at Berkeley, "Those behaviors are more damaging than anger. Anger is situational, while disgust and contempt are about the low worth of the person in general."

Tending a marriage

Once the realization is accepted that even between the closest human beings, infinite distances continue to exist, a wonderful living side by side can grow up. If they succeed in loving the distance between them which makes it possible for each to see the whole against the sky.

—Rainier Maria Rilke

A marriage needs tending to, or it will wither and die. I tend to my husband and marriage best when I am tending to my own needs first. Alan's happiness is important to me, but not at the expense of my own. I made an excellent choice when I married Alan, and so did he. We flow well together and balance each other most of the time. He tends to my needs as best he can as I do to his. He is my closest friend and most trusted confidante. I love him as a person apart and not just because he is my husband. We plan on growing old together if fate permits.

Women need to stop thinking that any one person is going to "complete" us. Only you can complete you.

But let's face it, some husbands and marriages are worth tending to, and others are not. Women are not raised to think this way. That's why women are more likely to lose themselves in marriage than men. All women, regardless of how successful or competent they are, can be vulnerable to losing themselves in a romantic relationship.

I learned this hard fact in my first marriage many years ago. I married at twenty, and the marriage lasted five years. The first two years I was, for the most part, a pitiable mess. It seemed to me that I could not breathe unless I was in the same room with him. I hated the way I felt, but it was as if I were in a drug-induced coma. Looking back, I now understand how I fell into such a state. I was living alone in Tokyo and had several years of high living already under my belt by the time I wed.

He, my ex, became my anchor and replacement for the family I missed. It was a strange kind of asexual relationship from the start, which made it even more dangerous. In my head, I made him into a god and my reason for living. I was busy working as a model, but everything I did, or did not do, was fueled by my fear of being away from him. I would not go on location unless I could be back by nighttime. I was made to look gorgeous in front of the camera or on the runway, but in my real life I let myself go in a bad way.

Any intelligent woman who reads the marriage contract and
then goes into it, deserves all the consequences.

—Isadora Duncan

Losing my way

The truth is he really had nothing to do with any of this. He did not demand or even subtly coerce me into surrendering myself in such a way. I did so freely. He was not uncaring, though he could be coldly indifferent. Did I forget to mention that he was Japanese, and thus not prone to displays of emotion? Of course, this emotional freeze made me even more nuts. This didn't change the fact that it was all about me projecting my needs and fears on this one person who just happened to be him. It could have been anyone, really.

I became increasingly repelled and disgusted by my own neediness. On occasion, I had fleeting moments of strength and clear thinking that soon evaporated, and I would once more descend into panic. It was exhausting to live like this. The end of this reign of madness came quite out of the blue. I was sitting next to him on a long flight back to Tokyo from London, and then it happened. A moment I had been praying for.

Lost in my thoughts, I turned to look at him. I looked at his sleeping face, the course black hairs in his nose, and his neatly manicured folded hands, and this is what I thought. *Who are you, this person that I have given up my very self for?* And then I started to gently and quietly weep. I knew I would leave him one day. On he slept while a new me was being born. Just like that. Right there in the sky, in the middle of the clouds. An ordinary unanticipated moment, and I came back to myself.

I love you, but I love me more.

—Samantha—*Sex and the City*

My love affair with me

At that moment, I made a solemn promise that I would never lose myself like that for another ever again. Didn't matter who they were or how much they professed to adore me. The thought of losing myself again was more terrifying than the thought of being alone. There were genuine moments of caring that I shared with my ex, but for the most part, it was not love that I felt, but fear. And that is not what love is about. I learned to differentiate between the two. I had to remind myself many times of this promise, but once that pact was made, there was no turning back.

When I first married Alan and moved to Los Angeles, everything was new and at times scary for me. I knew no one but him and the people I met through him. There were moments in those early months when I felt that old familiar insanity rush through me. The need to control, the fear of being rejected, the wondering what he was doing when we weren't together. It was all there. But so was my promise to myself. With it, a deep love for myself had begun to emerge that temporary madness could not destroy. I had learned that pain and joy begins and ends in my own mind, and that no one could fill my emptiness but me.

You do not have to give up yourself to love another.

We can all go a little insane when we first fall in love, and there is something wildly intoxicating about being drunk on love. I just have a strong aversion to the appalling withdrawal symptoms that seem to go along with it. When we love deeply, it always involves an element of risk. There's no way around that.

I tell Arielle to love deeply, even play the fool for love if she chooses, but always keep a part of herself that no one can ever take away. If a man asks that of you, then get as far away as you can. A partner can only take from you what you are willing to give away. And women, for various reasons, are wired to give away too much. Men are not immune to the tumultuous emotions and passions of romantic love, but yet they still don't seem to lose themselves the same way that women do.

Marriage is a great institution—but I'm not ready for an institution.

—Mae West

Real love empowers. It does not diminish or demean. In a marriage of equals we become more and never less than our finest self. We learn to set boundaries and establish a healthy flow of give and take. Your love affair with yourself is the most important and rewarding one you will ever have. If you find someone to love you in this same way, with all your flaws and darkness and beauty and goodness all fused together in your unique one-of-a-kind package, then you have indeed hit the jackpot. Doesn't matter what age you are—you have to know and love yourself first, and then you can give to another.

Making it work or calling it quits

When marriage works, it is a wondrous blessing that has to be nurtured and protected. For Alan and I, our marriage is like a third party that we honor regardless of whether we are getting along or feeling particularly *in love*. At its finest, marriage is a spiritual partnership where we help each other grow and become more of our very best. When we strip away the fantasies and illusions of marriage, we begin to experience it as the vehicle to our own deepest transformation. Together, with great care and tenderness, lies the opportunity to heal our wounds and brokenness.

Everything you need to work on in yourself will be magnified in marriage. And even though that work can only be done in the privacy of our own minds, the process is easier when we have that special love beside us. For Alan and I, our marriage is a safe and comforting refuge from a sometimes cruel and complex world.

If you are afraid of loneliness, don't marry.

—Anton Chekov

Like any relationship, not all marriages are meant to last. The end of a marriage can be extremely painful, especially when children are involved. But when it isn't mostly good, why stay together? When a marriage becomes cruel and abusive or a partner coldly indifferent, how can that be good for children? I believe children are happier when their parents are as well. The end of a marriage is not a failure, and you don't get graded. There is no pass or fail. In fact, it takes a great deal of courage to end a marriage when the love has died and the magic is gone.

Most of us arrive at marriage with high expectations and low preparation.

Over two million people married last year, and 50 percent got divorced. A recent study by the AARP shows that one in three U.S. marriages end in divorce, and women initiated two thirds of these divorces. That trend increases by a significant 16 percent in marriages longer than thirty years. Reasons for breakups vary, but a surprising many boil down to plain old unhappiness and unwillingness to settle.

Women may initiate divorce more than men, but men get remarried after a divorce or the death of a spouse quicker than women. My dad remarried two years after mum died, and Paul McCartney wed (and ultimately divorced) Heather Mills a little too soon after Linda's death for his daughter Stella's liking.

You may be his one and only soul mate and love of his life, but you can be replaced—sooner than you might like to imagine. It's just the way it is. I used to think that if I died first, I would not want Alan to be with another woman. I don't think that way anymore. If, after my death, Alan found a woman who he could love, then I would want that for him. I would want him to be happy. What we shared could never be replaced. It would have no reflection on how much he loved me, nor do I feel that my dad marrying Jean was in any way disrespectful to Mum.

It's just that men seem to need the comforts and company of a marriage partner much more than women. After a divorce or death of a spouse—especially if the marriage was difficult—many women learn to relish their new-found freedom after decades of tending a husband and family. Many would not trade this new taste of independence for the companionship of another partner.

In love with "being in love"

Being in love and loving are not the same. It is naive to expect to be "in love" with our marriage partner all the time. In a long relationship, romance may be intermittent at best. And at some point in any relationship, romance has to give way to reality. Bills need to be paid, groceries shopped for, and dirty laundry washed. If you are in love with "being in love," then marriage is not for you. The ecstasy and thrill of new love is bound to evolve, if we are lucky, into something richer, deeper, and ultimately more satisfying.

We make too much of romance in marriage.

At the very least, passion should last a few months, and two to four years at the tops, says research psychologist, Arthur Aron. Yet a marriage with no romance at all surely leaves one yearning for something more. Romance is still important for Alan and I, and we both take the initiative to be creative and keep the flame alive. Having time apart definitely helps, as does the good fortune of having world travel available to us both. But sometimes we still get stuck like any other couple. It takes focused intention because it is easy for a long marriage to become stale and predictable. When we think we know each other just a little too well, and there is no element of surprise and spontaneity left, boredom is inevitable.

Love at first sight is easy to understand, it's when two people have been looking at each other for a lifetime that it becomes a miracle.

—Amy Bloom

It's a wonderful bonus when we can find new life in the familiar, especially when it sneaks up on us seemingly out of the blue. Sometimes, I will look at Alan across the table drinking his morning coffee, intently reading the newspaper, and a warm rush of overflowing love will completely fill me up. When Whiskey died, another gift our furry friend left us was the reminder of how little time we have with our loved ones. It brought us both a renewed sense of perspective and appreciation for each other, and with it the awareness to not waste time on petty grievances and discord.

L' affair

The desire for romantic love can be very powerful and seductive. When we feel unappreciated and neglected, eyes can begin to wander and hearts pine. Even in a good marriage, monogamy can be difficult to sustain. To be with one person for years and have them satisfy all our needs is a tall order. Temptation can happen to anyone. It does not mean your marriage is doomed, and it does not make you depraved or wrong. It just makes you human. Temptation, however, does not necessarily promote action.

You meet someone new who makes you feel alive in ways your partner does not anymore or maybe never did. Being attracted to someone in this way may rouse parts of oneself that have long been buried inside. You feel euphoric and excited about life again in ways you haven't experienced in years. Feelings like this can be intense and disturbing and create turmoil in us and crisis in a marriage.

The desire to have an affair is usually an indication that something inside of us needs to be paid attention to. The place to start is an acceptance of these feelings and a willingness to look at what is going on beneath the surface. Being able to look honestly at these feelings, without judgment or guilt, can lead us to examine what may be lacking in our lives and our marriages. Any feelings we resist and deny have a tendency to become obsessive. That does not mean you will act on the urge to have an affair; it just means you stop moralizing about your thoughts.

Fantasy and reality are very different, especially when deeper issues are not being dealt with.

The idea of an affair can be exhilarating, but not knowing where such thoughts might lead may be scary and confusing. If you are lucky enough to have a partner you can talk about this openly with, it could be a breakthrough opportunity for you both to find ways to improve the partnership you are already in. Or it could become clear that it is time to end a marriage that has simply run its course. We also need to call upon our maturity to really think through the consequences and cost of giving into an affair.

My inner sex goddess

During the last eighteen months of my first marriage, it became clear that it was time for my inner sex goddess to emerge. She had been asleep long enough. There was not, nor ever had been, any real sexual heat between my ex and I. We were more like brother and sister than lovers, and at twenty-three years old, I was not willing to settle for that. As I grew stronger, I knew it was only a matter of time before my marriage would end. The on and off, year-long affair I began with a photographer was not the cause of the breakup by any means, but it did in its way contribute to it. The man and the affair was exactly what I needed at that time, and I inherently knew this.

People noticed how different I looked. I noticed how different I felt. I took care with my appearance, and for the first time in my life, I felt like a confident woman instead of frightened little girl. He made me feel like the most beautiful woman in the world. That could not be labeled wrong to me despite what anyone may have thought or said. I was too happy and alive to feel guilt or shame. It was a mature relationship. We both knew what it was and what it could never be. I was not looking for a serious commitment and neither was he. That would come later with Alan, and with it the end of my first marriage.

Some people claim that marriage interferes with romance. There's no doubt about it. Anytime you have a romance, your wife is bound to interfere.

—Groucho Marx

Chronic cheating is another story altogether, but even then, every couple has to find what works for them. We do not know what really goes on in the privacy of a marital arrangement, nor is it our business to know unless we are told. Some people are able to accept a marriage with the agreement of an open relationship. Very modern in theory, but for most people, the reality of that scenario is probably much more complicated and painful.

There are numerous ways that people cheat and let each other down. Deceit, indifference, withholding, and neglect are just a few.

According to an article in the *Los Angeles Times* by Pamela Druckerman, it's not that the French cheat more than Americans (despite the stereotypes, they don't); it's that when they do cheat they respond to it differently than most Americans. Druckerman further adds that "the French are apt to think of infidelity as one of the predictable pitfalls of marriage and don't assume that cheaters should be tossed out of the house." On the other hand, Americans seem to "get hung up on the 'lying' aspect of infidelity whereas the French are not as perturbed by a few discreet lies to preserve an otherwise good and solid marriage."

While it is true that an affair can be devastating to a marriage, and only a third of marriages survive an affair, it is also true that many marriages end not because of a betrayal, but because of a trail of unspoken hurts and resentments that accumulate over the years.

New rules

The challenge for most couples in a long relationship is how to grow together, and simultaneously expand and evolve individually. Marriage is a contract, and the rules of the contract should always be open to renegotiation for both partners. It's a work in progress, and what worked once may no longer work. That said, I think that if a couple agreed to monogamy, then they should both do their best to honor that vow. That, or they should make new rules that work for them both.

When responsibility and obligation start to feel like suffocation, it's hard to feel light and breezy with each other. A certain amount of surrender will be necessary from both partners, but smothering never works. If you try and control a mate out of fear, it can sometimes result in them doing the very thing you fear. But when we give our partner the freedom to exercise an option, more than likely they end up choosing not to. Possessiveness is about fear, not love. The kind of marriage where couples are joined at the hip isn't healthy for anyone. Mutually supporting each other's individual growth and freedom is. Chains do not keep a couple together—trust, self-love, and time apart do.

Security in a relationship lies neither in looking back to what it was in nostalgia, nor forward to what it might be ... but living in the present relationship and accepting it as it is now.

—Anna Morrow Lindbergh

Staying together

Alan and I have shared the intoxicating highs and on some occasions, the lows. Sometimes we both miss the urgency and intensity of the early years, but not the insecurities that went along with it. We are well aware of the rare intimacy we are privileged to share, and the exquisite comfort of being absolutely at ease in each other's presence.

What a delicious thing—to be able to enjoy each other's company without having to talk all the time. The closer we are, the more we can be together in silence. We guard this with our lives. With maturity and experience, we learn to maneuver through the inevitable peaks and valleys inherent in any marriage. We learn to discern between the normal consequences of a long relationship and the warning signs that something deeper is wrong.

There are always signs that something is amiss if we are paying attention.

The lack of alternative options is not a valid reason to stay married. We stay because of the kindnesses, forgiveness, gratitude, and comforting sense of being at home that a loving stable marriage gives us. The little things really do matter the most. It is the tender daily expressions of affection that keep us close when the responsibilities and stresses of life temporarily dim the flames of passion. The undivided, focused attention from the man she loves is more valuable to most women than anything money can buy. And this, it seems, is the very thing that many men have difficulty giving.

Men, I have found, are willing to listen when they are not being nagged at, and women will stop nagging when men clean off the bathroom sink without being asked, and remember birthdays, anniversaries, and other obligations without being reminded. When a man tells his wife to stop being his mother, the only reasonable retort is to say you will stop being his mother when he stops behaving like a child.

The Hallmark marriage

In twenty-eight years, I have learned a lot about marriage and even more about myself in the context of my marriage. I have learned that I am good at being married. I am a devoted and happy wife, on a part-time basis, that is. Don't get me wrong. The love I feel for my husband is a full-time thing. Always will be, no matter what. I cherish the life we share and all the memories we have created, and I believe we are stronger individuals because of what we have learned and share as a couple. I just think that being together all the time is highly unrealistic and vastly overrated. It's the syrupy, Hallmark version of marriage that holds no appeal to me at all.

Exceptionally fond as we may well be of our partners and children, there is a rich inexplicable peace and satisfaction that can also come in their absence.

Too much togetherness can snuff the life and vitality out of the best of relationships. For me, time alone is a nonnegotiable essential. It allows me the space to keep growing as an individual, while valuing the many blessings that are part of being a couple. I have learned to be self-reliant, and both Alan and I have been able to maintain a strong sense of personal independence while honoring the deep bond of our marriage.

This kind of arrangement is not for everyone, but I wouldn't have it any other way despite fierce initial resistance, and on occasion, frustration when Alan has to miss a special birthday or anniversary. At those times, we either celebrate before he leaves for a trip or when he returns. I have learned to be flexible. We don't relish long separations, but a few weeks apart now and then can do wonders for a marriage.

I also enjoy the quietness and calm order of my days when he's away, even though there are nights when I would give anything to snuggle up in his loving arms. I have had the time and space to grow into myself, with the added benefit of a partner who wants that for me, as I do for him. Plus, we have so much more to bring to our marriage when we are together. I'm not impressed when I hear people (it's usually women) boast that they haven't spent a day apart from their spouse in years, even decades. I feel sorry for them, rather than awed. But hey, that's just me.

But love … is more than three words mumbled before bedtime. Love is sustained by action, a pattern of devotion in the things we do for each other every day.

—Nicholas Sparks

I told you so!

Constant criticism is definitely a romance and joy buster. Blaming and incessant snapping is a form of contempt that can have a long-term negative affect on marital satisfaction. Every time we lash out, we kill off little pieces of love that eventually tear a marriage apart. Holding back when you want to say *I told you so!* can go a long way to create goodwill in your relationship. If you want romance and intimacy, let go of judging and lashing out. Or go see a therapist if there are some unresolved issues that are festering. If it's hard to control your snapping reflexes and those snide remarks keep on bursting forth from both sides, couple counseling may be called for.

Blaming your partner for everything that is wrong in your marriage is a sure way to send your marriage on a downhill spiral to divorce. And sometimes, as important as it is to communicate and talk issues through, it's even more important to know when to shut up and leave some issues well alone. Throw out the *you always do this* or *you never do that* lines because they will only land you in heated trouble.

Ego, pride, and the need to be right need to die in order for love, trust, and intimacy to thrive in a marriage.

Learn each other's style of communication so you can stop small arguments from erupting into full-blown fights. When Alan and I were first married and got into a fight, his need to talk it out or *nip it in the bud* (his words) before it escalated made me clam up and want to escape. The more he pushed, the more I would want to run away. Being British and living in Japan, I was not accustomed to talk about feelings and get them out in the open. He, on the other hand, was raised in a household of loud Jewish women where feelings and opinions were overtly in your face.

Over time and with lots of practice, we learned to relax with our different communication styles and intimacy needs. He pulled back and pushed less. I opened up and reassured him that my need for space to process did not mean I was turning away from him.

Mind games

People, especially husbands, frequently behave in ways we do not want them to.

It's tempting to want to try and change our partners once we are married, but it never works. It only breeds resentment and serves to distract us from the work and healing we need to do on ourselves first. Anger arises when we judge our partners for doing something wrong, or not behaving the way we want them to. A need or desire is not met, so we get angry and blame. When I notice myself start to get irritable or annoyed at something petty that Alan is either doing or not doing, I try to switch the focus back to me. I ask myself what is going on inside of me that is making me feel edgy and impatient.

145

I know from experience that it's usually more about my stuff than his. Neither of us wastes time on passive aggressive mind games. If something is bothering us, be it big or small, we say what needs to be said if it's worth saying. I've learned that a partner is not a mind reader. If you want something, learn to ask for it without blaming the poor bloke for not figuring it out first.

It takes strength and insight to know what we need and to be able to ask for it without attacking our partners. In an article in *O* magazine, Dr. John Gottman, who founded the Gottman Institute (otherwise known as the Love Lab), says the trick is employing what he calls a "soft start-up," which involves telling your partner, "what you need and giving them a way to succeed." An example he uses that touched my funny bone goes like this: instead of saying, "I'm sick to death of cooking dinner, you lazy slob," Gottman instead suggests you say, "You know, I'm sick of my own cooking. I think we need to go out to dinner, or have you take charge of dinner for a while." Hmm—food for thought.

All very well and good, but there are those days when you are tired and really bugged about something, and you just blurt out what you are feeling without thinking it through. Or as I have found, sometimes I do think it through but blurt it out anyway. I just don't know how it's possible for two people who are together most of the time to always get along. Sometimes, we just have to let off some steam even if an argument follows. Then it's a matter of how quick we can make it right.

> *Women hope men will change after marriage but they don't,*
> *men hope women won't change but they do.*

—Bettina Arndt

Stop nitpicking

Women, it seems, are experts at nitpicking and finding faults (maybe there's a chip in our brain that makes us that way), and in the past I have been no exception. I am somewhat different now. I am kinder to myself, so I am able to be kinder to my husband. We prefer to build each other up and acknowledge our goodness and strengths. It is a conscious decision. The world can do a fine job of tearing us down and making us feel small without our assistance. Like me, you might still have moments when your otherwise charming husband will do something that will bug the hell out of you. It might be a patronizing smirk in the middle of an argument that rubs you the wrong way, or the trail of clothes he leaves scattered throughout the house after you have just cleaned up.

Just because on occasion you may look across at your snoring, drooling husband who is keeping you up half the night, and you gasp and wonder who this person is you married, does not mean you made a mistake of gigantic proportions. Do not fret or panic. We all have such moments, and thank God they do pass. You do not, however, want to be in the car with us when Alan is driving, and I am in the passenger seat. I do not want to be in the car when Alan is driving, and I am in the passenger seat. His driving brings out the worst in me. Need I say more?

So what makes it work?

In our culture, we are obsessed with images and stories of new, hot, and steamy romance. We also want to be in the know about who's getting divorced and why. According to Janice Kiecolt-Glaser, a psychologist at the Ohio State College of Medicine, about a third of divorces occur after just four years of marriage. Apparently, to make love last, a couple has to get on track to success early on. We are not so interested in stories of mature love that endures over the long haul. It is not considered sexy or newsworthy, yet it is what most couples aspire toward, though few successfully achieve.

Weddings, especially celebrity ones, are as popular as ever. Desperate Housewife Eva Longoria's wedding in Paris and Tom Cruise's wedding in Italy got more media coverage than the war in Iraq. On July 7, 2007, otherwise known as 7/7/7, people flocked in droves to get married. Chapels in Vegas were sold out for months with Elvis impersonators moonlighting as ministers working overtime. Las Vegas issues an average of 120,000 marriage licenses each year. Why am I not surprised

Maybe it's not just about finding the right person; it's about being the right person at the right time.

that it also has the country's highest divorce rate? Numerically speaking, 7/7/7 is considered an auspicious and lucky day. As we well know, however, a big and fancy wedding is no guarantee of lasting, marital bliss.

Perhaps there *is* an element of luck or a quality beyond the realm of our understanding that makes a marriage succeed. How do we define that certain something that allows two people to magically mesh? For Alan and I, we have no doubt that there is something bigger than us that brought us together and keeps us together. This belief keeps us bonded in spirit when our egos and personalities try to pull us apart.

Like any couple, we have had our issues to work through in our marriage, but it never felt like a heavy burden on us. There was not a lot pulling against us. Being in sync on the small and larger issues in life has never been difficult for us, though we do on occasion get out of sync with each other.

The power of saying I'm sorry

Sometimes love is just not enough to make a marriage work, no matter what the movies may say. And love does mean having to say *I'm sorry,* many times in fact, despite what that silly movie *Love Story* would have us believe. Apologizing when I have been in the wrong did not come easy for me, but I am working at it. To Alan's credit, I will admit that overall he has been better at this than me. Why does apologizing make one feel so vulnerable and exposed even when we know we are clearly in the wrong?

About a month ago, during a time when I was feeling very stressed, Alan and I got into a heated argument about something and nothing. I think we were both feeling a bit needy and unappreciated for various reasons. The more each of us looked for justification for our feelings and needed to be right, the more heated the argument became (sound familiar?). After hours of going at it, we were both emotionally drained and increasingly distant from each other. Everything he said came out the wrong way—or at least that's the way I heard it.

I don't remember how we resolved it exactly—I think we both reached a threshold where we'd just had enough of battling each other. I was a sobbing crumbling mess, and at some point, I think Alan just saw that I was completely exhausted and worn out, not just from the argument, but from the life stress I was experiencing at the time.

We slept apart that night, but the next morning he came into the bedroom, cradled me in his arms, and said with great love and complete sincerity, "Last night I failed you miserably and I am truly sorry," to which I replied, "It's a new day and a new beginning." And we began again.

> *Marriage is our last, best chance to grow up.*
>
> —Joseph Barth

See the best in each other

Beyond the obvious qualities like trust and communication, I think maturity and a sense of humor are huge. Without them, how else can two people stay together through the myriad of challenging life experiences that we all encounter? Financial worries, aging parents, naughty teens, illness, and droopy boobs to name a few. Getting older together is not glamorous, but it can be funny if you look at it that way.

Shared tears and laughter lighten our burdens and open our hearts.

One time when we were soundly sleeping, I passed gas so loud that it woke us both up out of the deepest slumber. We couldn't fall back to sleep as we were laughing so much. This was certainly no cause for the self-conscious embarrassment that one would feel at the beginning of a new relationship. A meager trade off, you might think.

Alan and I have seen each other through our worst and lowest and still manage to see the best and highest in each other. We have raised a remarkable child together and mourned the deaths of our mothers. In our twenty-seven years together, we have been witnesses to each other's journey. We each have strengths that the other does not have, and enough differences in our personalities to keep it interesting without pulling us apart. He loves tales of alien abduction, really bad horror movies, and The Three Stooges. Let's just say my taste is a tad more refined.

We both understand the wisdom of separateness and solitude, though neither of us abuse that freedom. He has taught me, by his example, how to open my heart more. He says that my even-mindedness grounds him. Sharing the same spiritual practice has been invaluable and pulled us through many times. We've learned how not to push each other's button (for the most part) and the importance of having a jolly good laugh together whenever we can.

We cannot really love anybody with whom we never laugh.

—Agnes Reppelier

DEATH AND IMMORTALITY

Flesh is merely a lesson. We learn it and pass on.

—Erica Jong

Death is not a subject we in the Western world are usually comfortable discussing. We do everything we can to deny death, especially our own. We accept death as long as we can keep it at a distance. I heard a Buddhist monk once say that we need to get really comfortable with the idea of death, sort of like inviting death into our living room for afternoon tea, so to speak.

It's hard to live a rich, joyful life without coming to terms with the reality that we live in finite bodies that will, in time, perish and die. There's just no way around this fact. As we age and see death all around us, it becomes harder to push this truth aside.

My many years of meditation have helped me to understand that I am much more than the fleshy human shell that houses my soul. This belief gives me a great deal of comfort. If, however, your image of yourself is limited to the physical form, then your experience of aging and ultimately of death will likely be one of panic and dread.

> *There is only so much preservation of this human body that one can do, only so much time we think we can buy.*

Yes, it's hard to see the aging of our bodies, for we know deep inside that we are edging closer to death. Sometimes I stand in front of the mirror and dispassionately examine my face and body. I do all I can to maintain my looks, and I can, for now, pass for a woman a decade or so younger than I really am—or so I am told.

Still, I can see the loosening of skin on various parts of my body, but I also see a face and eyes that shine with joy and hands that remind me of my mum's. Despite good genes and excellent self-care, it is only a matter of time before I will start to look like the older woman I will be. If I am fortunate, one day I may be eighty. Even then, I'm sure I will still feel like the same old me on the inside, and I will enjoy looking back on all my *remember whens* of a life well spent and savor it till the very last breath.

This body is not me. I am not limited by this body. I am life without boundaries.

—Thich Nhat Hanh

I don't find it morbid or depressing to contemplate death. In fact, the more at ease I have become with death, the more I appreciate my everyday life. Time doesn't get wasted. I know that each day could be the last, but it's not a fearful urgency I feel. It's not like I feel pressured to fill my life with spectacular moments and huge life-changing epiphanies; it's just the awareness of how fleeting this journey is that makes even the ordinary moments seem extraordinary and life enhancing to me. Sometimes, though, this heightened awareness of transience does make me downright weepy, occasionally at the most inappropriate of times.

In our quest for the fountain of youth, we have become obsessed at trying to deter death from catching up with us.

Last week I saw an elderly, silver haired woman in the grocery store who I swear looked so much like my mum my heart almost jumped right out of me. I stood behind her in the checkout line, as close to her as I could get, as if to breathe her into me. I had to hold myself back from engulfing her in my arms.

Another time, I was sharing a rollicking moment of tearful laughter with my daughter when suddenly the poignant realization that this too, this perfect moment, will one day be no more. I don't know how many more times I will get to spoon with my husband in our bed at night, or how many times I get to sit side by side with Arielle while we get our toenails painted bright red. I drink in all these moments wholeheartedly while I can.

There is only one day left, always starting over:
It is given to us at dawn
And taken away from us at dusk.

—Jean Paul Sartre

Life is a continuum

Everything that has a beginning has an ending. I have made peace with this truth for the most part. The thing is, that although life can be painful and messy at times, it is also exquisitely rich and intensely beautiful. I have seen a lot of life through these blue eyes of mine. They've seen birth, death, and everything in between, and I'm in no hurry for it to be over. I am enjoying every moment of this wondrous ride and intend to continue doing so for as long as it lasts.

Sometimes I wonder what it feels like to be no longer in this physical body. Will I wait around to watch over my loved ones, and will they do the same for me? What will the moment of passing be like? I know I have been through this many times before and will surely remember it all again.

If you listen to someone describe a near death experience, you will hear over again how beautiful it is on the other side. So beautiful, that most people say they did not want to leave that glorious peaceful light and be brought back into their bodies.

Our real self, the soul, is immortal.
We may sleep a little while in that change called
death, but we can never be destroyed.

—Paramahansa Yogananda

We cannot outwit death

Friends frequently ask me if I'm afraid for my loved ones and myself when we travel. The answer is no. I am a fatalist, especially when it comes to death. I feel that when our time is up, it is up, no matter what you're doing. If it's not your time, then nothing can happen to you. I can strive to take certain, wise precautions and refrain from dangerous, risky behaviors, but even then, I could just as easily die walking across the street as I could sky diving from a plane. I find this approach to death frees me from useless worry over something I ultimately have no control over.

Years ago, my uncle Jim had just finished running a half marathon and was flushed with a sense of well-being and pride. Then, with a glass of sherry in his hand, he died in his favorite chair while his wife made a celebratory roast beef dinner. At 4:45 p.m. his wife had a husband; at 5:15 p.m. she was a widow. One morning, a friend in her late twenties was getting her two small children ready for school when she had a brain aneurysm and died minutes later. It was the last day that she would have breakfast with them. We all know stories like this, but can't imagine it ever happening to us or our loved ones. But it does, everyday.

Life as we know it can end in an instant

When we can begin to talk openly about death, these stories won't induce tremendous fear in us, but will simply serve as a reminder of how fragile our bodies are and how fleeting life is. I do sometimes wonder, however, if those who are about to die a sudden death know it on some level, or do they have no inkling at all.

When we wake up on any ordinary morning, apparently healthy and well, and have breakfast and take our showers, surely there must be something that whispers to us that this day will be the last. Could Uncle Jim have had any inkling he'd be lying in the morgue instead of eating his roast beef dinner? Did my friend have any sense that she only had one day left to get her kids ready for school?

Every exit is an entry somewhere else.

—Tom Stoppard

We may well have an intellectual and metaphysical understanding of death, but the pain of human loss can tear at our hearts with such force we may wonder what hit us. There is also, I recall, a sharp raw focus that we experience when we are in the midst of intense grief. In a somewhat unsettling way, all the heightened emotions I experienced when Mum died made me feel very much alive, even though it seemed as if I were moving through a dream.

As painful and sad as Mum's death was, it was also anticipated, and on some level a relief that she was no longer suffering. My mum was dead, but life would go on. How could life continue if my husband and daughter were taken away from me suddenly? I imagine that I would probably have to be heavily sedated, as such inconsolable grief would be bigger than I could contain. I wonder how one makes it through an hour with such pain, never mind a day.

I am not afraid of my own death, but I cannot begin to count the ways I would miss them both, the ones I love and trust most in the world. I fully expect that I would continue my daily conversations with them whether they were here with me or not. People will presume I am talking to myself and completely lost my mind, or maybe they might just think I'm talking to someone on one of those annoying cell phone things that fit over the ear. I think they call it a blue tooth.

On my birthday morning a few days ago, I sat for my usual meditation, and I felt a great longing for my mum. I was missing her so much and thought about the long labor she went through giving birth to me. Instead of pushing that thought and the tears away, I began talking to her. I told her how much I missed her and about everything that was going on in my life. I felt her closeness and just sat with her in stillness for a while. We often try and hide away our sadness, instead of holding it gently in our hearts.

O aching time! O moments big as years!

—John Keats

Only wisdom and love continues

No matter how much fame, fortune, and power one may gain in this lifetime, when we pass on, nothing goes with us but the depth of our wisdom and understanding. Nothing else. We may have our personal philosophies about what we expect after we die, but what happens after death is not as important as what happens during life. In a sense, life is a preparation for our death. I believe that when we die, we are shown a panoramic review of our lives where we get to experience a flashback of all that we ever did and thought. Everything, no part left out. This is not something to be afraid of, but it does remind us to live life with greater attention and gratitude.

According to Dannion Brinkley, author of *Saved by the Light,* our past life review will be experienced from a second person's perspective. In other words, as we observe our review, we become every person we have ever encountered. We will feel everything that the other person felt as a direct result of our words, actions, and thoughts. It reminds us that nothing in our life goes unnoticed. No moment and no interaction with another, however brief, gets left out.

> *Nothing is worth more than this day. You cannot relive yesterday.*
> *Tomorrow is still beyond your reach.*
>
> —Goethe

Start preparing now

If we desire to greet death with an open heart and peaceful mind, the time to start preparing is now. If we want to die well, we must begin to live well. How we live our lives from moment to moment will be reflected in how we experience death. That is why it's so important to take care of unfinished business while you still can. No more putting off till tomorrow when you may never have that chance again.

The difficult things need to be said, even more than the loving words that don't carry the same emotional charge and risk. It means expressing the anger in order to heal. It means letting go of all that separates us so we can come together in a place of love, if at all possible.

Other times, we take those closest to us for granted and don't take the opportunity to express our love as often as we could. It's sad but true. When our loved ones are alive and well, we're always a little too busy for them with something else that demands our attention. Then when they die, we would give anything to hold them tightly and tell them over and over how much we love them.

Life is very short and there's no time for fussing and fighting my friend.

—The Beatles

Tell someone you care about how much you love him or her. Go over to your husband right now, look into his eyes, and tell him. Tell those nearest to you, as often as you can, how much they mean to you. Then write that letter that needs writing, and make the phone call you have been putting off. You know what I'm talking about. The sister you feel distant toward, or maybe it's the brother you never got along with. Whoever it is, we all have them in our lives. Don't let things go unsaid. Where once there was a little wall to cross, time will build a bigger wall much harder to break down.

And then I think about all the strangers I meet on any given day—at the gym or the market, or maybe sitting next to me on the plane or at the counter at my local health food café. Do I take the time to share a few words or listen to their stories, or am I always in such a rush to get on with my own life? Sometimes when I am rushed and impatient, I remind myself to slow down and take a moment to listen, smile, and exchange a few words.

I think about the lifetime of disappointments we all carry and the sorrows we endure. I think about how similar we are underneath, and how a little love and kindness can make so much difference in all our lives. And I think about my life review, and how every interaction, however brief, never goes unnoticed. Can I be a little kinder and more interested in what someone has to say? Can I be more patient and understanding? And can I be forgiving to myself when I fall short, as we all do.

We are with those we have lost in material form, and far, far nearer to them now than when they were alive ... For pure divine love is not merely the blossom of the human heart but has its roots in eternity.

—Helena Blavatsky

Love is eternal

Without a doubt, I believe that the energy of love will always continue through the different realms of existence. I know that the love and deep bond I share with Alan and Arielle will endure beyond this physical world. It doesn't make sense to me that love just ends and is limited to only one lifetime. At twenty-three years old, Arielle still has a hard time talking about death. She says her biggest fear in life is losing her father and I. I tell her what I have always told her. I will be with her forever and for always—in the sun, the moon, the air, and the wind. I will come to her in her dreams and whisper to her as she falls asleep each night. I will blow gentle angel kisses over her face to soothe away her loneliness and remind her of my enduring love.

How would you live your life differently if you knew you had only six months left to live? Ask yourself this question, and see if it doesn't wake you up from sleepwalking through your life. If your answer is *there isn't much I would change*, then you are on track. If, however, the question sends you into a crazed panic, then you don't have a moment to lose to make some necessary changes in your life.

The veil that separates this life and the next is fragile and sheer.

What would you attempt to do if you knew you could not fail?

—Anonymous

This is it, right here and now. A lifetime goes by very fast. Life is no dress rehearsal for some future incarnation. Everything you need to know and all you need to learn from are right here where you are. We will never know when our time is up or when our days are numbered. God is the sole keeper of that appointed date. The time to start preparing is now. Not tomorrow or the next day. Invest yourself fully in the time you have right now, for that is all you ever have.

If we live in such a way, as if each day could be our last, imagine how different life could be. There would be no time to waste in fear, self-pity, and resentments. Only love, truth, and being awake would matter. All else would fall away. Imagine such peace and freedom. So wake up and don't let your life slip by. Live with this awareness until the very last breath, and you will then experience the exquisite joy of the beauty of aging.

Nourish Your Spirit

Books

Where There Is Light, by Paramahansa Yogananda (Self Realization Fellowship, 1988)

A Path with Heart, by Jack Kornfield (Bantam, 1993)

Wherever You Go There You Are, by Jon Kabat-Zinn (Hyperion, 1994)

The Enlightened Heart, by Stephen Mitchell (Harper & Row, 1989)

At Peace in the Light, by Dannion Brinkley (Harper Torch, 1995)

Gratefulness, the Heart of Prayer, by Brother David Steindl-Rast (Paulist Press, 1984)

The Highly Sensitive Person, by Elaine N. Aron, Ph.D. (Broadway, 1996)

Siddhartha, by Herman Hesse (Bantam, 1951)

Letters to a Young Poet, by Rainer Maria Rilke (Vintage, 1984)

The Seven Spiritual Laws of Success, by Deepak Chopra (New World Library, 1994)

The Prophet, by Kahlil Gibran (Knopf, 1923)

Finding Peace Through Pain, by Antoinette Bosco (Ballantine Books, 1994)

Dark Night of the Soul, by Thomas Moore (Gotham Books, 2004)

Many Lives, Many Masters, by Brian L. Weiss, M.D. (Fireside, 1988)

The Art of Happiness, by His Holiness the Dalai Lama (Riverhead, 1998)

Awakening—A Guide for Living with Death and Dying, by White Eagle (White Eagle, 2002)

Who Dies? by Stephan Levine (Anchor Books, 1982)